DEVEL(
EMOTIONAL HEALTH:
THE COMPACT GUIDE

No book can replace professional medical or therapeutic support, advice or treatment. If you are experiencing psychological distress, trauma or mental health issues, then there are some organisations you can turn to in the Resources section at the back of this book – but you should also consider talking to a doctor, medical practitioner or emergency services if you are in immediate crisis.

DEVELOPING YOUR EMOTIONAL HEALTH

THE COMPACT GUIDE

Andy Barker, Brian Cooley
& Beth Wood

NICK HERN BOOKS
London
www.nickhernbooks.co.uk

A Nick Hern Book

Developing Your Emotional Health: The Compact Guide
first published in Great Britain in 2024
by Nick Hern Books Limited, The Glasshouse,
49a Goldhawk Road, London W12 8QP

Designed and typeset by Nick Hern Books, London
Printed and bound in the UK by
Clays Ltd, Elcograf S.p.A.

A CIP catalogue record for this book
is available from the British Library

ISBN 978 1 84842 970 3

MIX
Paper | Supporting
responsible forestry
FSC
www.fsc.org   FSC® C018072

Contents

Introduction

Your emotional health is important. Our post-pandemic world is full of unrelenting challenges – and so being aware of your feelings, wellbeing, balance and contentment has never been of more significance.

This book is primarily aimed at supporting performers and creative professionals to develop sustainable emotional health – but, of course, it can be used by anyone wanting to develop their emotional health, regardless of their sector of work. It introduces a toolkit of techniques to improve, manage and maintain good emotional wellbeing. It offers practical strategies and tips for overcoming difficult situations, reframing negative thoughts and beliefs, and taking charge of the level and type of stress you choose to accept. It will guide you through the widest range of circumstances and enable you to build an array of positive resources that you can use to power your life and your creative work. We have aimed for a practical, relaxed and easy-to-understand book that is accessible and straightforward to use. The purpose is to support you in the direction of travel that you want for yourself and your sustained emotional wellness.

Between us three authors, we have ourselves worked in many different sectors of the creative and communicating arts, as performers, directors, writers, stage managers, educators, university lecturers and corporate leaders. We know from our lived experience what can happen when emotional health and wellbeing are adversely impacted by the commercial realities of the worlds of business and the creative industries. So in this book, we pay forward our shared and individual perspectives with one aim: *to support you to move purposefully in the direction of travel that you want for your sustained emotional wellness.*[1]

As defined by the Mental Health Foundation UK, 'emotional health is a positive state of wellbeing which enables an individual to function in society and meet the needs of everyday life'.[2] But creative professionals and performers often have to meet so much more than these 'needs of everyday life'. The life demands of being a creative can require astonishing quantities of patience, endurance and courage. And in times when we are already fragile, the creative process can easily tip us into the realms of mental ill-health. We don't have the luxury to choose when we are ready, or not ready, for being fully creative. And that is not the only challenge of being a performer or a creative professional.

The creative arts are frequently vocational, and this can create an employment environment that is not always optimised for the wellbeing of those working within it. We often feel as though we have precious little control over our careers. We have to learn to manage expectations without settling for second best in any way.

We have to cope with stress through what can be a brutal casting process; it's simply not possible to sail through every audition or interview and remain unaffected. We have to stay positive in periods of unemployment, to keep moving forward and learning wherever possible. We need to keep a vigilant eye out for some of the unhealthy negative emotions, such as resentment, anxiety and envy. We must be aware of the inevitable emotional pendulum swing, between the massive buzz of a good audience on a good night of a good play, and the emptiness at the end of a run or the anxiety of not having the next job lined up. All of these challenges make it even more important for us to feel resilient and empowered in our emotions and our lives.

Ideally the emotional resources should be in place for us to be able to call them to hand when we are in need: either when undertaking creative work or looking for our next engagement. And if we are in a transitory or protracted period of unemployment, the challenges of finding work, staying creative and simply surviving can sometimes drain us of every emotional resource we had thought to call our own.

This was one of the motivating reasons the three of us wanted to collaborate on writing this book: to support performers and creative professionals by sharing the scientific insights of our mental health, wellbeing and business-effectiveness company Mind Fitness Learning,[3] and its sister company Mind Fitness for Performers.[4] Every one of us should be able to enjoy the pursuit of what we love as creatives and not have to live a life of reduced fulfilment or limited satisfaction. This book provides a route map for harmonising your internal emotional balance, amidst the pressures and demands of working in the professional creative and communicating arts. In so many respects, creatives are used to trusting their imagination, exploring their emotions and coping with change. As such, you are already well placed to embark on this journey of what is possible.

All that you learn about good emotional health – having healthy emotions and regulating them effectively – can, of course, be applied to the characters you create. Learning to bring emotions from under the surface into the conscious arena is a technique that can be used in your rehearsals and performances. The entire concept of emotional intelligence is a rich framework to apply in your assessment of a character's ability to achieve what they want in the narrative they are placed in. This can be an effective tool to create dynamic tension in any performance, and it is certainly a way to enhance empathic engagement with your audience. By developing and upskilling your awareness and ability to implement emotional wellbeing insights, you will be making a useful addition to your creative toolkit.

How to Use This Book

We have structured the book to make it as accessible as possible. At any given moment we may refer to actors, performers, presenters or creatives, and we ask you to transpose any shared insights to your own relevant role or context. In some ways, whatever work we do, we are all 'acting' the part of the role we are currently playing in the organisation or group of people with whom we are working. Use your imagination to make the relevant leap.

If you're reading from cover to cover, the chapters move from concepts and key ideas about emotional health to an exploration of what makes up the holistic creative whole – brain, imagination and body – through to tackling specific aspects of your career, such as auditions, performance and periods of unemployment. Each chapter will stand alone if you are looking to deal with a specific challenge.

Chapters generally begin with a slice of learning, always evidenced by science, since understanding tends to bring a level of buy-in and commitment to the development process. When we deliver training sessions, whether live in person or online, they are scattered with a fair few 'Aha!' moments, where participants discover something about the brain or emotions that allows them to understand why they have always done certain things, or previously failed to change in the way they might have wished. We have tried to reflect this aspect of our approach, so insights are shared in sequence and at the appropriate time.

In each case, the scientifically supported learning is followed by practical exercises and techniques that employ a creative approach. Neuroscience tells us that our imagination and our medial prefrontal cortex – our higher-thinking brain – are closely linked. Building strong pathways between the two is one of the best things we can do for good mental and emotional health.[5] We will use our imagination through the process to sharpen and deepen our focused thought. In turn, this heightened focus will give rise to creative insights and feed into the work of being a more skilful performer.

The book concludes with a follow-up plan using all the techniques you have learned. Confidence comes from the knowledge that we have the ability to cope in a crisis, because of the mechanisms we have learned and our trust that they will work. Once you have worked through the book, you will possess a range of resources to draw upon to make you feel better. If a challenge should arise, which of course it will from time to time, your new habits of thinking and responding will stand you in excellent stead to cope in emotionally healthy ways.

It is possible that there will be moments of discomfort and personal challenge as you work through the book. These are, in fact, to be expected and quite normal. You will learn to move through these states and out the other side, and we will give you the necessary tools to calm your anxiety and manage these types of 'stay where you are' responses. As you may appreciate, it takes motivation to commit to evolving the understanding and regulation of our emotional responses to a level that serves us better.[6] By serving ourselves better, we will be more ready and able to serve others in their moments of need.

To record and support your journey towards sustainable emotional health, we recommend you download the accompanying workbook from www.nickhernbooks. co.uk/emotional-health-resources – or have a notebook to use for the purpose. Exercises that are referenced in the workbook are indicated with the following symbol 📖 and the number of the relevant worksheet.

Ten of the exercises work best as guided meditations/ visualisations, and are flagged in the book with this symbol 🔊 . You can access recordings of Beth talking you through each of the exercises at www.nickhernbooks. co.uk/emotional-health-resources, to allow you to press play on your device, close your eyes, and follow along with the instructions.

Finally, we are grateful for the generosity and inspiration from colleagues, friends and delegates that have informed the ideas we have shared in this book.

Andy, Brian & Beth

1. *Beth on...*
Your Emotional Health

We could define a state of wellbeing as feeling more calm, confident and happy. For a performer it must also include feeling creative, motivated and connected, perhaps even inspired. In this chapter, we'll take our first look at how you can feel better more of the time. It is a key concept – and we will expand upon and reference back to it as we move through each chapter.

Essential to the process of becoming healthier and happier is building your emotional resilience. But what do we mean by resilience? It's not the old-school definition of 'pulling yourself together' or 'manning-up', but something that's bound up in flexible and adaptive thinking, emotional intelligence, and the capacity to accept and even to embrace change.

We have noted already that actors, performers and those working in creative industries need to possess high levels of resilience. Let's do a quick exercise to get an idea of what this strong sense of resilience might look like, and why it's so essential for performers.

Exercise: Resilience for Performers 📖 1

- Make a list of five aspects of your professional life as a performer that require resilience – for instance, periods being out of work, bad reviews, last-minute auditions, and so on.

- Next to each of the five items on your list make a note of a specific example of when you had to cope with that challenge, and give yourself a score from 1 to 10 on how resilient you were at that time. Then make a note of what emotions you felt, and for how long the challenge lasted.

- We will revisit these situations a few times as we work through the book, but before we move on to look at what an emotion is and how to harness them to help us towards good emotional health, just look at your own answers for a couple of minutes. Are the resilience levels those that you would have expected? Do they vary widely? Do you know why? More on this later.

Emotions

You may be feeling a concern that to achieve a calmer and happier life it might mean suppressing your emotions. *This is not the case.* Not only do emotions give our world colour, texture and even purpose, but we fully recognise that they are the quintessential tools of your trade if you work in the creative industries. By the end of the book, we hope that you will see and value your emotions as a richer and deeper resource to be drawn upon and employed in performance, as well as in everyday life, both with a skilful control that boosts creativity and better mental health.

Negative emotions will no longer be controlling your life. When one comes along, you will know how to give it its proper weight and respect, but not get drawn to a place where it takes over and destroys that which is good.

Emotions impact our health, performance, wellbeing, motivation, sense of fulfilment, and ability to make effective decisions. They also determine the strength and quality of every relationship we make.

What is an emotion? Scientists disagree about how many emotions there are and, to some extent, on the description of what an emotion is. Here we are defining an emotion as a conscious or semi-conscious experience characterised by mental activity and a certain degree of pleasure or displeasure.

We are essentially an organic computer with 100,000 chemical reactions per second. Every emotion is induced by the release of a chemical or compound of chemicals instigated by our thoughts. So, by changing the way we think, we can release a different set of chemicals and change the way we feel.

The most frequently referenced emotions are love, hate, desire, anger, fear and envy, which collectively drive the majority of human behaviour. Emotions can last for decades, sometimes a lifetime, and negative emotions can lead to serious emotional and mental ill-health. Later in the book we will look at the ABC model used in Rational Emotive Behavioural Therapy (REBT) to reframe unhealthy negative emotions.

It may be useful to draw a distinction between emotions and feelings. Feelings are brief and episodic, often the fleeting awareness of the emotions that lie underneath. As we go through the book you'll get used to identifying the emotion that is giving rise to the range of feelings we experience, such as irritability, disappointment, insecurity and tension. This is the beginning of owning, understanding and realigning your emotions.

Exercise: Long-lasting Emotions 📖 2

- Begin by writing down two negative emotions that have lasted or recurred over a long period of time, and two that are positive. For each emotion write down when you first remember experiencing it, and a time when you experienced it strongly.

- Keep these answers to hand. They are the first step in the journey towards full awareness of your emotional responses and patterns, and an understanding of how these have impacted your life.

There is no agreement between emotional theorists on the exact number of human emotions. Most commonly accepted is somewhere around thirty, but some believe it is possible to identify hundreds, even thousands.

If we accept that there is a vast range of subtly different, nuanced emotions – let us say as many as there are countries on the earth – then many of us may not even be aware of which 'country' we are standing in right now.

There are two reasons for this. The first is that we are trained as children to recognise the 'biggies' – angry, unhappy and happy; sometimes referred to as 'mad', 'sad' and 'glad' – and many continue to rely on these throughout their adult lives. Coaches and counsellors often have to drill down, asking, for example, 'Exactly what are you experiencing when you say you are sad?' In my experience, even performers who are highly skilled at analysing the nuanced emotional states of characters they are portraying are likely not to have the same understanding of their own emotions.

The second reason is that our emotions are constantly changing (an emotion is energy in motion), so an in-depth understanding of how we feel demands a consistently high level of awareness and vigilance.

Exercise: Emotional Audit 📖 3

We're going to follow on from the last exercise to do a quick Emotional Audit, to get an idea of where on the 'globe' you think you are. We'll do another in the final chapter.

- Begin by drawing four columns like the table below or turning to the relevant page in the workbook:

Emotion	Level of Intensity	Experience	Possible Cause

- Now spend ten to fifteen minutes completing the table by listing every emotion you know you have felt (or think you might have felt) in the last week; the level of intensity with which you experienced it; whether it was a positive or negative sensation/ experience; and what you think might have caused it. Finish by putting a star by any of them that you are worried about.

Negative Emotions

There's a lot of evidence that the human tendency to suppress negative or painful emotions is, in fact, damaging. 'The tendency to avoid emotional suffering is the cause of all mental illness,' M. Scott Peck observes in *The Road Less Travelled*, 'we must face problems directly, and experience the pain involved.'

When difficult or traumatic events occur, experiencing the emotion is an important part of the journey to recovery; when we postpone that experience, we postpone the recovery. We cannot travel through an emotion and emerge on the other side without becoming intimate with it.

We are going to explore the important mindfulness practice of simply sitting with an emotion, and address the issues of mental noise: the myriad thoughts that clutter our mind.

The number of thoughts we have each day has not been pinned down by scientists, but it is likely to be about 60,000. You may be surprised to learn that only 5% of these are spent on the task in hand. The rest we refer to as 'noise' – largely past noise, where we dwell on what has already happened; and future noise, where we imagine future potential problems, creating little mental movies that often lead to worst-case scenarios.

What tends to happen is that one automatic negative thought (ANT) leads to the next, which leads to the next and so on. And before you know it you are on the downward spiral, you have lost ten minutes in negative introspection, and you are feeling low. If we have suffered some kind of loss or rejection, it's important to give time and respect to the emotion we are feeling. What that *doesn't* include, however, is letting your brain begin that spiral downwards.

An important mindfulness exercise is sitting with a negative emotion. Let's say you've just found out you haven't got a job you were hoping for. The exercise allows you to sit with the sadness without the automatic negative thoughts taking hold – for example, 'I'm always rubbish at auditions', 'I did a great audition, what planet is the director on?!', 'I'll bet X, Y or Z got the role.' It is only about allowing and experiencing the emotion.

Exercise: Sitting with an Emotion

It's best if you do this exercise when you are feeling a strong emotion, but if you want to try it now, remember a time when you felt one of the negative emotions you wrote down in the previous exercise.

- Sit comfortably with your back straight, your feet flat on the floor, and your hands comfortably on your knees or in your lap. Close your eyes and take three deep breaths, breathing in through the nose and out through your mouth.

- If at any time during the exercise any unrelated thoughts come into your mind, just let them drift gently away and bring your focus back.

- Be aware of any tension through the body – bring your attention to it. Simply allow the tension to exist.

- Focus in on the emotion you are feeling, without letting it spill into a tumble of negative thoughts.

- Focus in on any physical sensations associated with the emotion, and the impact of the emotion on your body.

- Breathe into the sensations you are feeling.

- Allow yourself ten minutes to focus in this way on the emotion. Understand that you are giving yourself permission to feel the emotion without judgement.

- As you come out of the exercise, have a moment of observing with curiosity what is flowing through your body. Then move back into an awareness of the physical sensation connected to the moment, what your bottom and legs feel against the chair, what your feet feel against the floor.

Acceptance and Understanding

Acceptance is the first stage of changing the negative into something more positive. That's why it's important to sit with the emotion. It isn't the emotion itself that does damage; it is all the negative thoughts around it. The effort of trying to suppress or escape from an emotion is colossal; often this acceptance will come hand in hand with a huge sense of relief. When both powerful emotions and negative self-talk (which we'll look at later in the book) come knocking, the vehemence diminishes significantly as you open the door and acknowledge them.

The second part is understanding the emotion. Because we are not generally taught to understand how emotions work, we instinctively think that they come along because of external stimuli. In other words, we believe that we feel the way we feel because of other people.

The key to change is understanding that we are absolutely, each of us, responsible for our own emotions. Both the problem *and* the solution are to be found 'inside' us. This is a simple but profound truth. Misery is optional. Happiness is optional. And, to a very large extent, if we are in control of our emotions (and by this we don't mean squashing down any that seem too painful to embrace) then we are in control of our lives. From this position of control, we can begin to carve out the emotional path that we wish to travel.

A Positive Mindset for Emotional Health

We mentioned before that of the approximately 60,000 thoughts we have each day, it is estimated that only 5% are spent on the actual thing you're doing at that moment. The natural disposition of the mind is to wander, and a vast proportion of the time it will get entangled in negative thoughts and self-talk, which will lead to negative emotions. Negative self-talk is the host of 'can't do' critical statements that we make up about ourselves.

The more time we spend in the default of 'wandering', the more chance we have of experiencing anxiety and depression. Instead, we need to find a focused mode, when the brain is engaged – and this is most likely when it is processing something interesting and meaningful.

You need to identify your goals, your beliefs and your meaning – and to bring these together in the centre of your life. People we have trained report that when this happens, everything becomes easier; they are able to spend more time in a state of 'flow'; they stop getting in their own way. We will look at beliefs in Chapter 6, and tie them into your values and goals in Chapter 9, but this is the time to focus for the first time on your meaning.

There are as many different concepts of what gives meaning to life as there are people, so it's important that you consider deeply what it is to you now, at this point in your life. It can be universal, political, philosophical, artistic or seemingly trivial – there's no right or wrong. What is it that gives meaning to your life? What gives you energy and purpose and perhaps a sense of real fulfilment when you accomplish a task that is linked to it?

Exercise: Finding Your Meaning 📖 4

You may already know what gives meaning to your life. It may be as simple and generic as 'performing'. It may be your friends or family. Or it may be incredibly specific – the achievement of an accreditation that you are working towards, for example, or taking your mother to her sister's house every Thursday night. Or perhaps it is conceptual. My meaning is focused on a passionate belief in inclusivity, and this is what has driven me, all my life. If you aren't sure, jot down a few ideas and try them out, in the following way:

- Get yourself comfortable and take four deep breaths. Now close your eyes.

- Focus your attention on what gives meaning to your life.

- Imagine whatever it is that you have chosen – or each of the options you are exploring. Let the object, person or concept become as clear, as beautiful, and as important as you can in your mind. Imagine it in whatever way would give you the most happiness or contentment.

- For example, if you are focusing on tackling injustice, you might move from a picture in your mind of every child having an education, to a world where absolute equality simply exists and always has. Just think about the exciting ways you might visualise that!

- Or, if you said your meaning was derived from your family, you might move from a group picture of your children or siblings smiling to separate images of each of them finding something deeply fulfilling in their lives.

- Write down (or draw!) what the clearest, brightest, most inspiring version of your meaning looks like, and the emotions that you experience when you imagine it.

For the next two or three weeks, revisit this exercise whenever you can, so that it gradually comes to take a more important place in your life. Each time you revisit your meaning, make sure that you allow yourself the time and space to feel the positive emotion attached to the mental 'movie' you have created.

When we look at your goals later in the book, we will ask what our lives would look like if we achieved emotional wealth. By looking first at meaning we are also asking what our lives would *feel* like. It ensures that the vision you have in your mind is personal and, above all, authentic.

This is particularly important for performers. A life that is based around goals, beliefs and meaning attains the kind of quiet assurance that we attribute to Eastern philosophers and Buddhist monks. It is very far from the need to impress. And yet in a performer's life, the necessity of impressing cannot be escaped. A life with meaning has to be built carefully, consciously and compassionately. It can be done.

The process of integrating the different 'selves' that we have created over the years is also key. We have worked with many actors who have developed an almost separate private and personal persona. The public persona is brimming with confidence; but most do not see the 'person' they become as they exit the stage or finish the run of the play. Some can step into a party and become the confident performer, while others can do it only on stage. If this duality applies to you, then integrating the two (or more) versions of you will be an important part of the process towards good emotional health. Thinking about meaning is an important first step towards being happy and comfortable in your own skin.

We are going to look at the qualities of Happiness, Gratitude and Compassion, and consider their role in our journey towards emotional wealth.

Happiness

Happiness has long been the Holy Grail for Western society – the quality that we're all said to be searching for – but that status has usually meant it can only be dreamed of or, at best, planned for.

Hunting happiness is a trap that it is easy to fall in to, and you find yourself saying, 'I'll be happy *when* I own a car... *when* I earn more money... *when* I land a job at the RSC.' But one of the most important messages of this book is that you can be happy *now*. And more than that, you *deserve* to be happy now.

A recent study by Oxford University found that happy employees were 13% more productive, so increasing our happiness levels can help us to step away from intolerable pressure and achieve more.

Every chapter of this book will teach you to embrace positivity and move you closer to the state of emotional health. It doesn't mean that you pretend that bad things don't happen – acceptance is absolutely at the heart of all transformation; it is practising rational thinking through a lens of optimism. We can *choose* to have a good day. We can *choose* to celebrate our successes. We can *choose* to be happy.

There are two techniques that help us move towards a state in which we are choosing to be happy more of the time. The first is training ourselves to acknowledge the negative when it appears in our lives, but not to dwell on it, and of course not to move into the spiral of automatic negative thoughts. The second is to practise gratitude as consistently as we can.

Gratitude

Gratitude is at the heart of mindfulness – which we will explore in the next chapter – and it really does have the power to stop us being dissatisfied with our lives. It is impossible for our mind to think a negative thought *and* to be grateful at the same time. If you ever find that you can't dispel a powerful or negative emotion, simply concentrate on something you are sincerely and profoundly grateful for, and it will do a lot to dissolve the hurt or anxiety.

And it really is incredibly simple. It is beginning the practice of noticing what you do have, instead of what you don't. It's something that's certainly easier if you are living a simple life. I experienced this when I spent a little time in the jungle a few years ago. When the trappings of modern life are stripped away, it is possible to be grateful for *all* that you have, *all* that you do. In the modern world, with our overfull lives, there are a million things each day to be grateful for. You won't manage to be grateful for all of them, but mindfulness practitioners work towards engaging in deep and continuous gratitude. It's good to focus on just a few things to start you off.

Exercise: Daily Gratitude Practice 📖 5

- Begin each day by thinking about three people in your life for whom you are truly grateful.

- End each day by writing in a gratitude journal or notebook three things that happened during the day for which you are grateful. There is space in the workbook for the first three days – which should give you time to find a dedicated journal or book to keep using.

- Try to steer away, if you can, from being grateful for possessions.

Compassion

Many psychologists believe we are approaching a loneliness epidemic in the Western world. Finding a way to cure this would do much to alleviate the current crisis in mental health. We have an innate human desire to be needed, to feel appreciated, to see that our special qualities are understood and validated by others. For many, it comes very close to our meaning – and is therefore vital to our mental and emotional health.

We also know from neuroscience that, to a large extent, we become what we give our attention to. This is because our brain will always default to the neural pathway, the way of thinking, that we use the most. If we allow uncompassionate thoughts to fill our mind then we evolve into this version of ourselves. But because of neuroplasticity we can change our thoughts and beliefs. We can choose to evolve into the *best* version of ourselves.

The spiritual gurus across the world and across the centuries that have advised us to act only in love have been proved right. And there is yet another reason why it will make you feel better. The 'high' we get when we eat a bar of chocolate comes from a release of the chemical dopamine. An act of compassion (for example, doing what you can to help a charity you believe in, or giving up a night out to help a friend) will give you a dopamine hit several times the strength.

Exercise: Seeing a Friend with New Eyes

- Spend the first ten minutes when you next meet up with a friend (or speak to them on the phone or online) listening to them intently, as if you haven't seen them for years.

- It is likely that in response you will see them letting go of tension in their shoulders and face. If you can't see them and are only listening, observe the changes in their breathing.

- Notice the increased level of engagement your friend has in the conversation and the strengthened connection with you and your feelings.

- Observe changes in the language they are using, in vocabulary and sentence structure. Notice any increase in abstract or conceptual language coming from a freedom to express ideas.

- Then think about how you would describe the emotional shift you have witnessed.

- And finally, notice how these changes are making you feel. All of us experience a burst of happiness when we make someone feel better.

Emotional Intelligence

Almost every industry and sector has now accepted *emotional* intelligence (or Emotional Quotient/EQ) to be of equal – or higher – importance than IQ (Intelligence Quotient), the traditional measure of intellectual ability. For no industry is this more true than ours, where awareness of self and others, and the ability to create relationships, both on and off stage, largely determines the success of the whole endeavour.

The American psychologist Daniel Goleman set out five main areas that now form the basis of leadership and personal development work in numerous organisations, and drive the social and emotional learning programmes in schools that have been adopted in many countries. These are self-awareness, self-regulation (sometimes called emotional control), motivation, empathy and social skills. We'll look at each one in turn, and then revisit them to understand and audit these areas of emotional intelligence in Chapter 6.

Self-awareness

Self-awareness is a key component of emotional health and wellbeing, although it is worth pointing out that this is not the same as self-analysis or critical introspection, which can lead you deeper and deeper into the damaged parts of yourself. There's a lot of awareness work throughout this book and we ensure that this focuses on the 'whats' rather than the 'whys'. All the work we do is *future-focused*.

Exercise: Developing Your Self-awareness 📖 6

A common self-awareness exercise you can try now is simply to list your strengths and weaknesses, but we're adding in that you must write down *two strengths for every weakness* – and you must end your list by writing down a strength.

Self-regulation

Self-regulation encompasses many of the techniques that you will learn throughout this book to manage, rather than suppress, your moods and emotions. The aim is to be able to consciously determine how you will respond to any situation.

For performers, it is related to flexibility and responsiveness, which are key creative skills. It is also related strongly to responsibility and personal accountability, even to your moral compass.

Exercise: Exploring Your Self-regulation 📖 7

- Make a list of all the values you hold dear, with some words about why they're important to you, and with a star next to any that would be central to your code of ethics. As an example, mine would begin with 'Diversity: differences should be valued and celebrated so that each person feels able to be their true and authentic self.' (This would definitely have a star.)

- Once you have made your list, make a note of how each value can make you feel. It is likely that it will span the extremes. When I walk into an organisation that is practising (not just professing) diversity, it fills me with joy. When I work with an organisation that is excluding rather than including, I find it really hard. It is probably when I have to manage my emotions most consciously.

Motivation

Motivation, you will find, improves greatly as you move through the process of developing your emotional intelligence. You will find that it will no longer be there only on a good day, but woefully missing when you most need it. Instead, it will be a constant, helping to drive you forward. Being positive and hopeful – and remembering the meaning behind the tasks you undertake – is central to remaining motivated.

Exercise: Building Your Motivation 📖 8

Motivation to do something depends on whether you want it enough, whether you know you can do it, and if you believe you deserve it.

- *Whether you want it enough:*
  Your motivation will largely depend on how closely the task in hand is linked to your meaning. The more it matters to you, the easier it is to keep working to achieve something. Make a note on a scale of 1 to 10 of how important three tasks that you are currently undertaking are to you, and then try to increase the number by focusing in on why they are important.

- *Whether you know you can do it:*
  Your motivation will also depend on whether you actually have the skill-set required and, just as importantly, on whether or not you believe that you have that skill-set. Again, make a note on a scale of 1 to 10 of how equipped you feel yourself to be for each of the three tasks, and then try to increase this number by reflecting on similar things you have done or achieved in the past.

- *If you believe you deserve it:*
  Your motivation will depend on whether or not you have a robust and positive self-image. Make a note on a scale of 1 to 10 of how much you feel you deserve to accomplish the tasks, then increase the number for each, by listing the positive things you do or qualities that you have.

It's also worth knowing that willpower decreases through the day, so it is best to do the things that need real motivation earlier on.

Empathy

Empathy is not about feeling what another person feels, but understanding *how* they feel. It is possibly the most important of the five skills of emotional intelligence, as it is central to our ability to make and sustain effective relationships. Performers are used to walking in the shoes of the range of characters that we inhabit, and yet it's often something we have to train ourselves to do in everyday life.

Exercise: Expanding Your Empathy 📖 9

- Watch an episode of a TV soap or drama, focusing on only one character. Watch their body language closely, pay attention to their tone of voice, subtext and all non-verbal communication.

- After you've watched the episode attentively, close your eyes and for five minutes move through the action of the episode in your imagination as if it is *happening to you*. Concentrate on the emotions and all sensory experiences.

- Finally, tell the story aloud (perhaps record it on your phone if there isn't a friend to hand), or write it in your workbook, as if it is happening to you.

- Next, do the same when you get home from a meeting with a friend, describing the events and emotions they have been experiencing, as if they have happened or are happening to you. Notice whether your level of compassion for the person changes.

Of course, to empathise with anyone, the most important thing is to be deeply and genuinely interested. Again, this genuine interest is something that can be cultivated by simply giving anything our focused attention. By doing this we tell our brain that we have a reason to care.

At some point in their careers, most performers will have accepted a role that they did not initially feel drawn to, to find that they have fallen in love with the character once they have thrown themselves into the work. In fact, it is only our interest that makes anything extraordinary.

Social Skills

Social skills centre around effective communication. In many of the exercises you've been exploring, you have been learning to listen more deeply – using skills you will probably already be employing in a professional context – and you are learning to be reflective and to transform negative emotions into positive ones. These are key components to maintaining healthy group dynamics and achieving successful conflict resolution. You're also learning to better appreciate others and to work instinctively with compassion, making open and honest dialogue more likely.

Exercise: Enhancing Your Social Skills

- As a start, commit to giving genuine praise to at least three people each day. Tell your colleague they were great in Act Two today. Let your partner know the lasagne was excellent. Tell the busker that their song reminded you of a very special time. So often we register these things, but we don't say them.

- Remember that not all praise is spoken. If a toddler runs into your legs and you smile at their parent, you have told them non-verbally that you think their child is spirited and lovely. (Of course, if you have tutted, the opposite is also true.) It's a very simple technique that can really change lives, both theirs and yours.

Exercise: Intensifying a Positive Emotion

- Sit comfortably with your feet flat on the floor and hands on your knees or in your lap. Close your eyes. Take four deep breaths, breathing in through the nose and out through the mouth.

- Focus on one of the positive emotions you listed in the Long-lasting Emotions exercise (see page 16). Try, if you can, to feel the emotion; for some this will mean recreating the situation in your mind. Be aware of how the emotion is affecting you physically – perhaps you may be smiling.

- Give the emotion a colour, and let the colour fill as much of your body as possible. Now imagine that the emotion is becoming stronger and more intense. Allow the colour to change if that feels right.

- Hold the feeling and the colour for two or three minutes. Now relax, again taking four deep breaths to complete the exercise.

Often, we can intensify an emotion fairly easily by giving more attention to it. It's how a negative or painful emotion goes from 1 to 10 in as many seconds. But while we are horribly aware of the painful emotions, we often give very little thought or focus to those that are positive. We're either hurting or we're anxious or we're 'okay' – but by intensifying a *positive* emotion you will boost your sense of wellbeing.

It is a creative exercise similar to others you may be used to doing – for example, imagining your character's emotional journey through a scene or play. If it is an emotion that you are experiencing rather than recalling, you can also use gratitude to strengthen this feeling.

Conclusion

Humans have a natural disposition to hold on to the negative. It's natural, because our brains give priority to threats that may jeopardise our survival, and we respond to these threats with negative thoughts and emotions. We have to work to change from a 'cup half-empty' to a 'cup half-full' perspective on the world – but it can be done.

You are responsible for your own emotional health, which means that if feeling good is something you really care about, the change is within your power. And as we journey towards better mental and emotional health we can change more than our internal landscape. Imagine what the world would look like if everyone practised active, compassionate empathy; a world in which we made ever more and ever deeper connections.

Stay observant, stay appreciative, and stay curious. Gradually you can achieve the wonderful change from mind-wandering, where one automatic negative thought leads to another, to mind-*wondering*, where our focused attention brings interest, curiosity and awe. And it can change your life.

2. *Beth on...*
Your Resilience

We started looking in the last chapter at our resilience as performers, but it's important to spend more time exploring and developing it, as it underpins our ability to cope with the inevitable challenges in life, to bounce back after difficult events and situations.

As we observed, old-school resilience was very much the dreaded 'man-up' approach to life: 'What doesn't kill you will make you stronger', and so on. We know now that this rigidity creates an armour-plated shell that can mask acute internal fragility. New-school resilience is based on flexible thinking, the ability to adapt to new situations, to bend without breaking.

There seems to be a direct correlation between the level of scrutiny that people feel themselves to be under and the level of stress they feel. It is unsurprising that being a performer can be viewed as a stressful profession, with every choice laid out for public scrutiny. To create artistic work that is worthwhile we must dig deep, drawing upon our most intimate experiences and fragile resources, and then we must be prepared to take all criticism impersonally once we have laid ourselves bare to strangers and our performance becomes the topic of discussion.

The list of situations that cause stress is extensive – from coping with stage fright and audition nerves (and then, of course, the week spent waiting to hear if you've got the job) to the anxiety related to getting the next one. It's rare that this anxiety only comes into play once a job is drawing to a close; it's far more likely that the pressure of the next job will be playing on your mind and triggering those automatic negative thoughts almost as soon as the current job begins. Another huge cause of stress is the constant change as you move from contract to contract – unless you do a very long run, which comes with its own stresses. Add to this the financial instability and the lack of clear career progression, and it's a heady mix that is highly likely to be impacting your emotional health.

Exercise: Creative Stress Audit 📖 10

- Reflect for a moment on the level and nature of stress you are currently feeling.

- Imagine that you are a character and about to be portrayed in a film by a hugely accomplished actor. The exact stress that 'you'/the character are under is incredibly important to the plot and tone of the film.

- Your job is to close your eyes and get in touch with exactly what that stress is. What does it feel like? How does it impact your emotions and behaviours? It is an exercise that enables us to see our situation a little more objectively, from the outside, without getting tangled in the victim-complex that negative thoughts so often lead to. It can particularly help if you are a performer who is better at acknowledging and analysing the emotions of a character than your own.

- Now write down the character's (i.e. your own) stresses and strains, giving the actor who will be playing 'you' full and clear instructions about what the pressures are, and perhaps how to interpret and perform them (i.e. how they manifest themselves).

You might, for example, give details of a background stress that has been there for as long as you can remember, which results in a low-level tension and irritability. You might say that above this is an explosive stress that is linked to fear or paranoia, most often repressed but dangerous when it bursts through.

This is the level of detail we are likely to apply to the characters we play, but rarely to ourselves.

Exercise: The Surprise Visit 📖 11

- Imagine that you are performing in a new West End or Broadway show. The cast was told in rehearsals that a big casting director would be attending the fifth performance of your run. You have now been told that their availability has changed, and they will now be coming tonight to the dress rehearsal.

- Start by thinking of a non-resilient response to the situation, such as 'This is a complete disaster!' or 'This is so unfair!' Make a note of the emotions that you experience. Either write it down or shout it out, whichever works best. Then take three deep breaths to 'clear' this mental and emotional state.

- Now imagine a resilient response, as resilient as you can make it: 'It's not a perfect situation, but it's okay' or 'It is still a great opportunity.' Again, make a note of the emotions you experience.

This exercise shows clearly that it is not the situation itself (the same in both cases), but our level of resilience and our *response* to the situation that determine our level of stress and ultimately the consequence. It also introduces the concept of good stress, or 'performance buzz', as your resilient response may have involved a measure of excitement! We'll return to a similar high-pressure scenario in Chapter 9.

Performance Buzz

When we are training business managers and tell them that not all stress is bad, this is often received as a revelation. Not so with performers, who already know that a certain level of stress can be harnessed for a good purpose. From the time of our first school play, we understand that our pre-show nerves, the adrenalin, are a necessary ingredient of a focused and energised performance.

In fact, many actors report a sense of confusion and even distress when they are ill or exhausted and suddenly without the nerves that would usually power them into the show. I had this myself after an all-night tech in which almost everything went wrong. There wasn't time for a dress, so you would have imagined we would all have had extra nerves for the first night. But there were none, and without them many of the cast were simply without energy. The level of exhaustion made it hard even to notice this unusual state, or to care.

Humans need a certain amount of pressure to be fully engaged, to approach a task with full concentration. Again, this is why having a strong meaning is so huge – and to feel this pressure, first we must *care*. We must have an emotional connection with the task. It is why long runs of a production can take us to the bottom left of this chart.

The Stress Curve

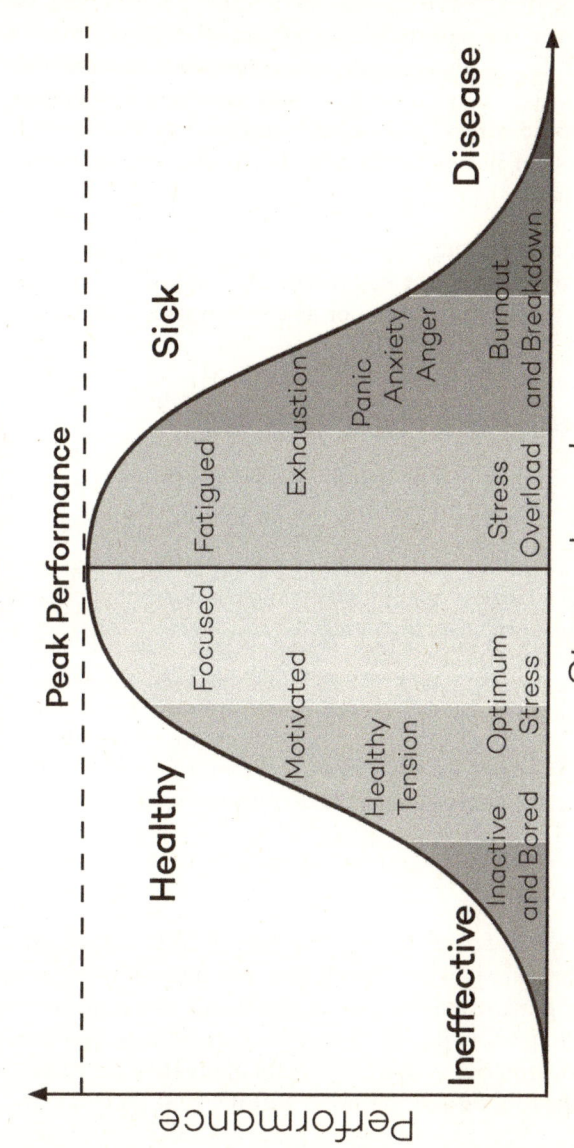

This bell curve clearly shows the place where we can deliver the optimum performance: right in the middle. Too far to the left on the graph and you are not fully engaged. Too far to the right and you are tipping into chronic stress, exhaustion and patterns of mental and physical ill-health. In fact, prolonged chronic stress can be fatal.

It seems clear that if you want to deliver your best performance, it is key to ensure that you are operating at the top of the curve – or as close to it as possible.

Exercise: Top of the Curve 📖 12

- Grab a few coloured pens if you have them. Make a note of the colour you are using for each cross.

- Draw a small cross on the curve for where you think you are (or were) in your current (or most recent) performance.

- Draw on two or three more crosses for other recent work.

- Put a cross that relates to the last time you felt that you were on the optimum performance line. Think about why.

Of course, our levels of stress – and our performance buzz – are just as important to our daily lives as they are to our performances. One of the things that tends to happen with performers is that you may sense this increasing pressure, but you are in a state of creative flow and do not want to let go of the buzz. But it's vital that you do.

If you use, for example, one of the mindfulness techniques that follow, you can quickly bring down your level of the stress hormone cortisol and pick up at the place you were. Too much 'ploughing on' and you will be unable to think clearly or to create. You are likely to feel that you are turning in work that is of a higher standard than it actually is.

The Stress Response: Fight or Flight

Here's the science behind the frustrating fact that you won't be performing at your best. If you draw an imaginary line into your brain from your eyes and another from your ears, the two places these lines intersect in the brain each side is called the amygdala. In normal circumstances the job of the amygdala is to pass sensory information up to the prefrontal cortex, the higher-thinking brain. But in times of perceived threat or danger it has another function: it initiates the 'fight or flight' response.

Most people can probably think of what this feels like. There is a surge of adrenalin (and other chemicals) through your body that gives you enough physical energy and strength to fight a wild animal should it be hurtling towards you, or to turn and run.

This instinctive response has served humankind pretty well through its evolutionary development. However, our brain works on a system of threats and rewards. If it senses a threat, then the 'fight or flight' response will kick in, even if it is simply one of the many commonplace stressful situations of modern life. Even more important is that once the 'fight or flight' response kicks in, then the amygdala no longer passes information up to the higher-thinking brain. At the times when you most need to be thinking clearly – when you're problem-solving, decision-making, or during an interview or audition – you simply can't.

It's key to learn techniques that you can use to get yourself quickly out of 'fight or flight' mode and back into a position where you can do your best – and one of the most important techniques is mindfulness.

Mindfulness

Mindfulness is the process of bringing your attention into the present moment in order to experience life more clearly and more fully. The evidenced benefits are emotional control, reduced levels of stress and increased motivation. As we've mentioned, mindfulness is deeply connected to acceptance and gratitude, and can bring you to a new appreciation of life, perhaps a life based on 'being' rather than 'doing'.

Once you've established a daily practice, you will enjoy a fresh relationship with any activity, from taking a shower or eating an apple to attending an audition or giving a performance. Mindfulness holds that every activity is worthy of our full attention, and if we find that it is not, then we should change the daily activities that make up our routine. If you evoke a genuine interest in every daily activity, you will have evoked a genuine interest in life.

Mindfulness buys us the time in which we can choose how we respond to a difficult situation. It helps to break through our deeply embedded resistance and habitual, long-held defences. We lose our dependence on reactive behaviour and break the chain of repeated behaviours. It provides a lens that allows us to see through our pretences and illusions – and, of course, it is a powerful way of learning to develop the necessary skill of focused attention.

Getting through our tasks quicker is not an objective of mindfulness, but it certainly is a result by default.

Anyone wondering how they can fit in daily practice only needs to do it for a few days to realise that you gain far more time than you lose. And as we said earlier, more focused attention brings about more frequent and greater moments of creative insight.

Preparing for Mindfulness

When you are doing any mindfulness exercise, it is important to prepare. Begin by sitting up tall in a straight-backed chair. Your spine should be held with the muscles relaxed around it. Place your feet flat on the floor and feel yourself centred. Your arms can be on each knee or in your lap, as you prefer. Always begin by using your physical frame to connect to the moment. Take a minute to be aware of the weight of your feet on the floor and of the places where your body is in contact with the chair.

Once you are ready, close your eyes and take four deep breaths, slightly longer than usual, breathing in through the nose and out through the mouth.

In the exercises below, you will be guided to think of or to imagine specific things. If other thoughts come into your mind, let them gently drift away without judgement, and bring your attention back to the present. As you get more practised, start to learn to notice these thoughts without getting caught up on them, and then let them go. When you finish the exercise make a note of any thoughts that were persistent. It may well be an issue that needs your attention. But for now, it is enough just to let any thoughts, any noise, go.

Here, then, are three of our favourite and most effective mindfulness exercises.

Guided Exercise: Image Breathing 📖 13 🔊 1

- Prepare for the mindfulness exercise as above.

- Start by locating an image, a picture of something in your mind that you find calming or reassuring.

- Now attach this image to the breath, breathing in and out four times. My image is a wave. I imagine a beach where I am standing in the water. As I breathe in, the water gathers around me. As I breathe out, I use my breath to push the wave up onto the beach.

- See the image that you have chosen clearly in your mind.

- Inhale and exhale four times, breathing in through the nose and out through the mouth, keeping the image clear in your mind.

- We do four breaths because this is the time it takes to slow the heart rate and begin to bring down the level of the stress hormone cortisol.

- Write down – or, better still, *draw* – the image that you chose so that you can return to it again.

Exercise: NOW

This exercise can be done anywhere, it's so quick and straightforward. It can even be practised before – or *during* – a challenging audition. It's a mnemonic so it's easy to remember:

- *N – Notice.* Stop whatever you are doing and notice whatever your focus falls on. This can be anything: the ticking clock, a mark on the wall, the shaft of sunlight on the floor.

- *O – Observe* in detail whatever it is that you are looking at.

- *W – Wonder.* Feel a sense of wonder about whatever it is. Everything is fascinating and even extraordinary if you look at it closely and with fresh eyes.

Guided Exercise: Foxhole in Your Mind 📖 14 🔊 2

This exercise is similar to the Russian theatre director Stanislavsky's sense memory exercises, which you may be familiar with.

- Imagine a place that is both safe and beautiful. This is your own personal foxhole. I have recently changed my own safe space from an underwater Egyptian city to a place in the Peruvian jungle that I was lucky enough to visit recently. It can be a place you know well, a location from a book, film or game, or simply a place conjured from your imagination.

- Visualise as much detail as you can – the shades of colour, the textures or smells, the temperature, the qualities of sound.

- When you are ready, place yourself into the setting, imagine yourself moving through the physical environment.

- What can you see in your near and peripheral vision? Is it warm or cold? Are the smells strong or subtle? What does the air feel like against your skin?

- After two minutes, open your eyes.

- Make a note of your safe and beautiful place – and how it made you feel. Or draw it.

This exercise works very quickly to slow down your heart rate and lower your levels of cortisol. With practice, your foxhole becomes a place that you can escape to whenever you feel the 'fight or flight' response start to kick in. If you do it enough times you may well be able to beat the symptoms of the stress response. We will return to this exercise later in the book.

Being in the Moment

Most of us live so little of our lives in the moment. Often it takes something extraordinary or overwhelmingly beautiful – like a sunset that takes our breath away – to take us to the wonder of the present moment.

Having said that, we have found that performers are used to immersing themselves in a journey from beginning to end, and will often come very close to staying in the mindful present throughout a performance. We are also often good at keeping our attention on a play that we are watching, or a TV show or a film. Newcomers to mindfulness exercises often report an intense sensation of 'waking up'. Others report a new ability to see both the big picture and the small picture at the same time. These are obviously great skills to have as a performer; many great actors are long-term meditators.

Mindfulness is the journey from effort to effortlessness. With practice there comes a continuous, ever-present flow that becomes our way of negotiating the world. It is about recognising the web of interdependence, the power of interconnectivity, as a new identity. As human beings and performers we are not only individuals; we are also a connected species with untold collective potential.

We commit to stop giving authority to aversion – by this, we mean that we commit to rid our thoughts of the habits of complaining, of judging, of seeing the worst in people and situations. And the way we do this is through gratitude. It is not an easy task and may take a while, but you can train yourself to notice that your cup is quite considerably fuller than you had realised. Think for a moment of the effect that attaining that would have on your levels of stress and your daily emotional health. It's important to work towards.

Exercise: Waiting

We often find that one thing performers are not very good at is waiting, perhaps because so many feel that key aspects of their career and life are not wholly in their control.

- On a single day, find at least five opportunities to wait: wait for the kettle to boil or wait at the supermarket checkout.

- During this time, know what you are waiting for, and simply wait. Don't let your thoughts move into the past or future. You are in the moment and, in that moment, there is nothing to do. Just wait.

Another skill to work on as a performer is decision-making. Often actors are incredibly good at collaborative decisions, which is vital for the creative process, but sometimes less good at making decisions on their own, or for themselves. Indeed, many find it a stressful activity.

Exercise: Decision-making 📖 15

- Try to be aware of as many decisions that you are making as possible in a day, and note these down.

- For each one, however small, use your creativity to imagine the consequences of two different paths, and then make your choice.

- Once you have chosen what you're going to do, stay strong. Do not allow yourself to revisit the path (or paths) that you did not choose.

When we look at neuroplasticity (the brain's ability to rewire itself) in Chapter 3, we'll find out that the more our brains get used to consciously making small decisions, the more easily they can deal with the bigger ones when they come along.

Mindful Performers

Mindfulness practice has an almost immediate effect of putting you more closely in touch with your senses, which is of course incredibly useful as a performer. It also helps you attain full presence and to have this in your conscious control. It means, for example, in long runs where the innate nerves have fallen away, you can consciously create the emotional state necessary to do your best work.

The more you practise mindfulness, the more you will gain a vigorous clarity on the way you see events, which can be taken into your creative process. Try to take a mindful stance towards all aspects of your work. For example, if you're learning your lines, sit straight-backed, take four breaths first, and read slightly slower than usual.

Notice the words, the sounds, the emotions that each phrase brings into your body and your voice. Try using the mindful practice of dissolving, of allowing things to pass, which is a key component of the transitional nature of the industry for most performers.

Exercise: Dissolving 📖 16

- Spend a day noticing all the things that dissolve away: sugar in tea, clouds in the sky, leaves falling from a tree.

- Note these down – or draw small sketches if you prefer. Pay particular attention to the last moment of clarity before the dissolving process begins, and the moment of completion as the final element disappears.

Try to use the process to let go of your character at the end of a long rehearsal or after a performance. It's also a useful device in terms of pushing the 'clear' button between tasks or between areas of your life. You finish a rehearsal, you leave the character, you step outside.

And finally, and most importantly, make the most of the connective nature of the mindful approach. Mindfulness helps to develop this acceptance, moving through non-judgement to a place where everything about each individual is fully valued. The collaborative potential, if a company is willing to work in this way, is enormous.

Exercise: A Seven-Step Process to Combating Stress

A key part of developing your resilience is knowing how to address stress when it arises, without falling back on a 'fight or flight' response. Here's a step-by-step process for you to practise when it next happens:

1. Recognise the signs of stress. It might be a churning feeling in your stomach or a general increase of tension through the body; perhaps a clenching of the jaw or pain between your eyes. There's myriad ways that stress will affect each individual. Try to identify the physiological symptoms that come most often to you.

2. Step away from your own signs of stress with one of the mindfulness exercises already described. Later in the book we will be asking you to build as much change as possible into your life – but a notable exception will be having one mindfulness exercise that you can go to whenever you need to bring yourself quickly out of the 'fight or flight' response. Choose the exercise that you like best or that you find calms you most easily. Do this exercise several times a day if you can, in order to train your brain to default to this exercise and the calmer state when required, without effort or conscious choice.

3. Look at the stressful situation and accept it. Consider the events that led to the stress. Concentrate on the 'what' rather than the 'why'. *What* happened? Look objectively, without remorse or any other emotional response, and, most importantly, look without judgement. You cannot accept if you are judging.

4. Commit to change. Know why this is a situation that you want to do something about. Relate it to your meaning if you can. On a scale of 1 to 10, how much do you want this change? (Remember we can want the 'small things' a great deal – for example, to eat more healthily or to be on time.)

5. Make a positive affirmation and speak it out loud: 'I can choose how I respond to this situation', 'I can make my diet healthier', 'I can improve my punctuality.' Say this out loud as many times as you can in a minute. We will look again at affirmations when we do the Inner Critic, Inner Cheerleader Exercise in Chapter 10.

6. Imagine a positive future. Later we'll look in detail at the human predisposition to create negative mental movies of all the things that could possibly go wrong. Creative people, of course, tend to be especially good at this self-torment! But we can use the same creative abilities to our positive advantage. Imagine yourself in three, four or five years' time (as feels best), having entirely solved this problem. What does this look like? And, more importantly, *feel* like?

7. And finally, a very important habit to adopt and nurture: always congratulate yourself for overcoming a stressful situation, for solving it, or at least for taking a big step in the right direction. In life, generally we so often miss the moment when something has worked. Performers are often criticised for being in love with applause or success. We have rarely found this to be the case. In fact, on the contrary, there is a real tendency to breathe a sigh of relief at the end of a run rather than giving yourself an enormous pat on the back

and properly reflecting on a job well done. If we are to walk towards a state of better emotional health, it is certain that we must all work harder to recognise and celebrate our successes.

There are a few steps we will add in as we work through this book. In Chapter 3 we'll learn to reframe negative beliefs, which can go a long way to releasing long-held stress. In Chapter 6 we will look at our cognitive bias and see if this is contributing to continued levels of stress. And we will look in Chapter 10 at setting and attaining goals that are in line with our beliefs and meaning.

Planning forward is not the same as negatively projecting forward, and it is key to ensuring that you spend as little time as possible on issues that are not contributing to developing your better emotional health.

Conclusion

Remember that stress depends on your perceived ability to cope with an event or situation. The way that you choose to respond is in your control. In fact, there is research that takes this even further, suggesting that those who have physical symptoms of medium to high stress but do not believe that this will damage them – instead seeing it as their body preparing to help them deal with the situation – do not go on to suffer.[1]

If we *choose* to see a situation, however difficult, as a challenge to be overcome, then to a very large extent our brain responds accordingly and delivers the chemicals and hormones to help us in the task. Never has the maxim 'We can do it if we put our mind to it' been more true.

3. *Andy on...*
Your Brain

My Story

At the age of thirteen, I joined a local community theatre company. It was an amazing set-up, based in a small purpose-built theatre and run by an innovative artistic director who had ambitious aspirations on the breadth of work that should be undertaken.

I first signed up for acting classes and I quickly added movement and technical theatre skills to the list. It was an absolute immersion into theatre and I was hooked. Every waking moment of my day, when I wasn't in school, was spent there.

I enjoyed acting. I was cast in more plays and shows. Small parts at first, but then bigger roles as age and opportunity permitted. When a part wasn't available I was happy to be backstage. I loved it all. I knew that this is what I wanted to do as a career.

By the time I was fifteen, I was being tipped as a potential talent. A big fish in a small pond. The artistic director met with my parents, and he urged them to support the idea of me going to drama school to train as an actor. He offered to coach me and liaise with the local authority to ensure that I received a full grant. That was possible then, and it all seemed too good to be true. What an opportunity. I should have been ecstatic. But I wasn't.

I felt the pressure starting to mount. Almost imperceptibly at first – and then the growing feeling that I should do as suggested principally because I owed it to those who supported me in continuing the journey. I realise now that I was doing it for them, and not for me. I was expected to succeed, and that was starting to build into unhealthy pressure.

I enjoyed the freedom of performing as an amateur actor in an amateur environment. I was under no pressure. I could experiment, make mistakes and fail without feeling judged. My new world would be one of harsh scrutiny and constant evaluation. And that terrified me.

I started to become ill. Gradually at first and certainly not seriously, but enough to impact my life as a young man. I experienced bouts of nausea. There was no pattern. It could be whilst walking in the street or eating a meal. In fact, in almost any scenario I could feel the waves engulf me. Strangely, I was never actually sick, but the nausea would crash in and render me helpless. Between bouts, I dreaded the next, never sure when I'd be crushed again.

The notion of drama school faded along with my health, but such was my love of the theatre that I persevered along another route that somehow seemed less onerous: repertory theatre. In the mid-1970s, weekly and two-weekly rep companies were still drawing audiences throughout the UK. I managed to get a job as an assistant stage manager (ASM) at an established weekly rep company and set off with a new-found sense of purpose. At that time, many people used the rep system as an alternative to drama school in which to develop and learn their craft.

The bouts of nausea still troubled me at times, but I enjoyed stage management and soon moved to being 'on the book', running the show and cueing the various technical elements. As the season was coming to a close, I was given a small part in a play and set about learning the lines. Rehearsals began and the nausea returned with a vengeance. The small number of lines wouldn't stick. I'd await my entrance and feel the sickness well up.

I was aware that the company was made up of established jobbing actors who exuded confidence gained from years of experience. I knew I could learn from them, but at the same time I felt increasing pressure from what I suppose now would be called 'imposter syndrome'. Of course, I was an imposter. A rookie placed in a world of talent and competence. What I couldn't see at the time was that I was being permitted to learn, to slowly nurture and grow. It was okay to be less than brilliant, and to welcome constructive criticism in order to develop. The pressure I felt was mine and mine alone. I was getting in my own way, but I simply could not see that.

I told no one, suffering increasing anxiety about the illness and my perceived ineptitude. I was miserable, existing on minimal food and kaolin and morphine (a preferred stomach-settling medication at that time) from a bottle I carried with me at all times.

I must have delivered an adequate performance as the company asked me to return for their panto season as acting ASM. I had a small role in the chorus and a brief appearance at the end as a named character. It was hardly taxing, but to me it became torture. Lines would simply disappear. Time onstage was spent panicking that I was going to be sick. I felt wretched. At a point in my life when I should have been having the time of my life, I was filled with fear every day. I dreaded performances and became anxious to the point that I was unable to function.

In desperation I saw the theatre company's doctor. He listened attentively and diagnosed stress. I was prescribed tranquillisers and I went on my way. I was furious with him. I had asked him to treat me for the constant sickness and regarded this as a misdiagnosis. I took the medication and felt just as sick but now more spaced out, which added to the challenges I was experiencing. I soon stopped taking the medication.

I'd reached a crossroads, and realised that enough was enough. Things needed to change. I made a decision that I've never regretted. I decided to stop trying to be an actor and concentrate instead on stage management. I was tired of trying to please others, though I no longer knew who. My decision was a revelation, a release. Almost instantly I felt better. Pressure fell from my shoulders. My head cleared. I had a new objective, a path that felt right for me.

The doctor was, of course, right. I had experienced stress. In fact, I had actually been living with acute anxiety. It was one of the reasons I set out to understand more about stress and mental health, and to follow the career path that I am now on.

I see now that I self-sabotaged. I did it to myself – it wasn't caused by my theatre colleagues, or the youth-theatre director, or my parents. I applied the unhealthy rigid pressure myself. My own beliefs and thoughts triggered my stress response, and I tumbled out of control.

The Stress Response

As we said in the last chapter, we all need a degree of stress and pressure – the performance buzz – to function and to perform well, such as when the nerves kick in before a show. In a steady state, stress is experienced as pressure that drives and motivates. It flows in cycles, and can often be felt or expressed as excitement.

But when we experience threat or danger our stress response kicks in with a 'fight or flight' response. At moments of genuine danger this is great and necessary; however, the flaw is that our brain cannot distinguish between a real or imagined threat. In our modern world the perceived threats are of a different nature. You have already made a list of some of them that apply to you (see the Creative Stress Audit on page 38).

The stresses we experience can be more constant. We are bombarded with information in our 24/7 society, where it feels like everyone and everything is always 'on'. We perceive threats everywhere. Our stress response is constantly alerted. The amygdala becomes overactive, with serious consequences to our mental and physical health. For many this means that we stay in a state of constant anxiety, with little or no information going up to our higher-thinking brain. We are unable to restore our rational thought processes.

When I struggled to remember a few simple lines and felt ill, I was in a state of fight or flight. I thought I was feeling anxious about being sick, but I know now that I was feeling sick *because* I was anxious. I had no knowledge then that I could help myself. In fact, it was always in my power to do so. We can change!

Neuroplasticity

Our brain has an amazing ability to rewire itself. This process is called neuroplasticity and it is the reason why we are able to develop new mindsets.[1]

The brain is made up of information connections called neural pathways. Every time we do something new – like learn a skill, such as juggling – a new pathway is created, and with repetition the pathway strengthens and becomes robust. When we change a habit gradually, over time, a new pathway is formed and strengthened whilst the old pathway weakens. With concerted effort and practice, we can form and strengthen new pathways and bypass the old pathways, therefore changing the way we think, along with the way we feel and behave.

Practice is key. We have to repeat – and keep repeating – the new thought or activity, because if we lapse, the brain will take the most familiar route and re-establish the old unhelpful connection. With repetition and practice, however, our new connection becomes established.

Science tells us that we don't have to continue being a worrier, or someone who fears flying – or auditions. We can train our mind to our advantage. We can identify the unhelpful beliefs and attitudes that trip us up and then we can begin the process of change.

Beliefs and Attitudes

Our thoughts and beliefs define who we are. We hold numerous beliefs about ourselves, about others, about the world around us. Many of our beliefs serve us well. They motivate, inspire and positively guide us.

However, we also hold beliefs that serve us less well. We may not be aware of them, or if we are, we defend them as our truths, regarding our beliefs as an intrinsic part of who we are. I see now that the unhelpful beliefs that I held all those years ago resulted in my self-sabotaging behaviour.

Our belief system is built from experiences gained from times of early childhood. Our parental and family experiences, our schooldays, and our cultural and socio-economic influences all serve to create the mindset we hold and defend. They are our truths. Beliefs form the guiding principles, and we uphold them as though they are the laws of the universe. The power of our beliefs is enormous. When they serve us well, that's great; but when they don't, we may be blissfully unaware or simply accept the 'flaw' in our personality.

But we can develop the insight and willpower to formulate more helpful and rational alternatives. Here's how...

Understanding Your Beliefs

It's the irrational beliefs we hold that cause us to get in our own way. An irrational belief is rigid or extreme; it is not sensible, or logical, or based in reality. The following are examples of irrational thinking, and we will look at these in more detail in Chapter 6.

Rigid beliefs: A rigid belief tends to contain 'Must', 'Have to', Should' statements. For example: 'I have to be liked by everyone I meet.'

Awfulising/catastrophising beliefs: We catastrophise when we think a situation is 100% awful, completely terrible, and cannot be any worse. For example: 'It would be absolutely awful if any member of the company didn't like me.'

Low-frustration-tolerance beliefs: 'I have to be comfortable at all times. I cannot bear being uncomfortable.' For example: 'I couldn't stand knowing that a member of the company didn't like me.'

If I knew at the age of twenty what I know now, I would have understood that my own irrational, rigid, catastrophising beliefs stood at the root of my problems. I had developed rules based on demands of my own making, that asserted the rigid personal belief of 'I *must* succeed as an actor otherwise I'll let people down.' And closely tied to this was the catastrophising belief that 'It would be *awful* if I don't succeed and it will mean that I'm a useless person.'

The ABC Model

The central element of Rational Emotive Behavioural Therapy (REBT)[2] is the ABC model.[3] This is used in therapy and coaching practice to examine our beliefs, to identify the behaviours and emotions that come from them – and to manage the irrational ones.

'A' stands for the *Activating event* or *Adversity*. In other words, the thing that happened. The situation.

'B' stands for the *Belief* – namely, the belief or beliefs that you hold about that situation.

And 'C' stands for the *Consequence* – how we react, feel and behave as a result of this belief. The consequence can be broken down into how it impacts our *emotions* (does it make us anxious or angry?), our *behaviour* (did we storm off shouting angrily?), and our body's *physiology* (did we feel sick and start to sweat?).

Because we are not always aware of our own unhelpful belief/s we may adopt a stance that's known as 'A-to-C thinking' where we omit the B – the belief. Here's what A-to-C thinking would look like:

A = Activating event/Adversity:
'The director shouted at me because I'd forgotten my lines.'

C = Consequences:
Emotion: 'I feel anger and anxiety.'
Behaviour: 'I shout back; say things I didn't mean in order to get my own back; and storm out.'
Physiology: 'I experience a pounding heart and feel flushed and tearful.'

But the activating event and the consequences do *not* lead from one to the other, without a series of irrational or rigid beliefs, unconsciously held, between them. And it is these beliefs that have created a consequence that will most certainly lead to more problems in an already tense situation. You might explain the event as 'The director shouted at me and made me really angry' – but was it really the director who *made* you shout and say things you later regret? Or was it the beliefs you hold? Such as the following:

A rigid belief: 'You *must not* shout at me.'
An awfulising belief: 'It would be *awful* if I were shouted at.'
A low-frustration-tolerance belief: 'I *cannot stand* being shouted at.'

In other words, the rigid beliefs that we regard as our personal laws have tripped us up, and have led us to consequences that won't be helpful for the situation, for others, or for ourselves, including our own emotional health.

Here's how our beliefs are ultimately unhelpful in this situation:

A rigid belief: 'You *must not* shout at me.'
We cannot possibly apply our law to others. We have no control over others' behaviour, only our own.

An awfulising belief: 'It would be *awful* if I were shouted at.'
Would it be truly 100% awful if you are shouted at? Really? In the grand scheme of things, it's undesirable, but not a catastrophe.

A low-frustration-tolerance belief: 'I *cannot stand* being shouted at.'
You can't stand being shouted at? Again, it is, of course, undesirable. But is it something you literally 100% cannot stand?

Finally, by adding the beliefs into this scenario and not skipping directly from Activating event to Consequence, the picture is more complete:

A = Activating event/Adversity:
'The director shouted at me because I'd forgotten my lines.'

B = Beliefs:
'You *must not* shout at me.'
'It would be *awful* if I were shouted at.'
'I *cannot stand* being shouted at.'

C = Consequences:
Emotion: 'I feel anger and anxiety.'
Behaviour: 'I shout back; say things I didn't mean in order to get my own back; and storm out.'
Physiology: 'I experience a pounding heart and feel flushed and tearful.'

My ABC

I wish I'd been introduced to the ABC model all those years ago. I could have identified the true situation with my irrational beliefs and had an opportunity to change them – and the outcome.

My beliefs then were complex and varied. This is an example of an ABC formulation that applied to me at the time.

A = Activating event/Adversity:
'I forget my lines and feel sick.'

B = Beliefs:
'I *must not* forget my lines. I *must not* let people down. I *must not* be sick.'
'It would be *awful* if the cast saw through my lack of experience.'
'I *cannot stand* the prospect of being seen as incompetent.'

C = Consequences:
Emotion: 'I feel anxiety.'
Behaviour: 'I become self-protective, quiet and withdrawn and want to run away.'
Physiology: 'I feel sick and experience sweating, a dry mouth, a pounding heart and memory lapses.'

This is, I believe, a fair representation of what was happening in my head at the time. At the forefront was the belief, the demand, that I *must not* be sick. I saw that as my overarching fear; a dread of being exposed; and shame, an emotion we'll explore in Chapter 6. My fear stopped me seeing that it was my irrational, extreme beliefs that were triggering my anxiety-based nausea.

Changing Our Beliefs

So, how do we start the process of change? In Rational Emotive Behavioural Therapy, the system is called *Disputing* – so it becomes the ABCD model.[4] By applying the method of Disputing, we are able to put our belief through a rigorous testing process where we identify, explore and challenge each belief. We look for evidence to support whether a belief is helpful to us, or not.

The process requires us to ask ourselves the following questions about each of our beliefs:

1. *Is it true?*
2. *Is it logical?*
3. *Is it helpful?*
4. *Would you teach your belief/s to others?*

The belief, once opened to scrutiny, may fail on all or some of these criteria. That will be enough to know that it's advisable to develop a new, less rigid, more helpful belief.

So, let's revisit the beliefs that I held and that tripped me up all those years ago, and employ this disputing process.

1. *Is it true?*

'I *must not* let people down.'

Is it true that you absolutely and categorically must not let people down? Do you have control over how others think, feel and behave? How will you know? Are you able to read their minds and know that your perceived failure will result in them feeling let down by you?

'It would be *awful* if the cast saw through my lack of experience.'

Would it actually be awful? How does this situation compare with awful situations? Is it as bad as a severe life-changing injury or even death? It's not ideal certainly, but is it truly 'awful'?

'I *cannot stand* the prospect of being seen as incompetent.'

Although it's not a prospect to welcome, is it true to say that you absolutely 100% cannot stand it? It's not what you'd choose, but whilst being unpleasant, you could stand it.

Result: The belief is *untrue*.

2. Is it logical?

'I *must not* let people down.'

Again, you have no overall control over others' thoughts, feelings and reactions. It is illogical to suggest that your actions will definitely result in an imagined outcome.

'It would be *awful* if the cast saw through my lack of experience.'

Is there logic in asserting that this imagined scenario will be absolutely awful? No.

'I *cannot stand* the prospect of being seen as incompetent.'

Is it logical that this (even if true) would be utterly intolerable?

Result: The belief is *illogical*.

3. Is it helpful?

These beliefs are creating the barriers that are tripping us up; in my case, creating the obstacles that made me unwell.

Result: The belief is *unhelpful*.

4. Would you teach your belief/s to others?

These beliefs created enormous problems for me and negatively impacted my life.

Result: Absolutely not!

Time then to reframe our beliefs. But into what?

We're seeking to reframe our thinking into beliefs that are more rational, and that can pass the disputing questions. Our rational beliefs are flexible and non-extreme, reality-based, sensible and logical.

A flexible belief is the opposite of a rigid demand, so instead of the 'Must', 'Have to' and 'Should' statements, we change them to preferences: 'I would prefer that...' Non-extreme, reality-based beliefs are non-awfulising and non-catastrophising.

Here's an example of another ABC situation. There's another potentially stressful Activating situation, but having rational, flexible, non-extreme beliefs leads to happier consequences.

A = Activating event/Adversity:
'I am onstage understudying a role for the first time.'

B = Beliefs:
'I *would prefer* not to let people down, but I cannot control their response.'
'I'll do my best and hope that it's good enough.'
'I'll learn every time I'm onstage. It's what I'm here to do.'
'If the cast do see my inexperience, I hope they're supportive and give me constructive feedback. It's my time to learn.'
'I *would prefer* not to be seen as incompetent. However, I am better than that, and I can stand to be coached and mentored by experienced actors.'

C = Consequences:
Emotion: 'I feel concern.'
Behaviour: 'I am motivated to channel the nerves, face up to situations, push on and learn from every experience.'
Physiology: 'I feel nervous but in control.'

Of course, this is a theoretical example, and makes the process look easy and quick. To be able to master the ABC process requires self-awareness and honesty. It also requires practice.

Remember earlier in the chapter we mentioned neuroplasticity? The process of rewiring the brain, with repetition, takes about six weeks.[5] With time and practice we can create and embed new flexible beliefs. For this reason, your intellectual understanding of this process will, with time and practice, become an emotional understanding. When you're truly *feeling* it and *living* it – then life really changes.

Conclusion

You don't need to live with your unhelpful beliefs and suffer their impact on your life and your career. That's what I did and it seriously disrupted my life. I was feeling sick because I was stressed. I thought I dreaded going to work for fear of feeling sick, 'exposing' myself and being shamed. I was actually fearful of failure and adverse judgement. I was stressed because of my rigid, demand-based beliefs about failing and disappointing others.

I may never have made it as an actor. I may not have possessed the talent or the drive required. I'll never know. And that's absolutely fine. Things turned out well and I'm very happy and enjoy a full life, thank goodness. I could have spent the rest of my life regretful and bitter, churning around the narrative that I was unlucky and robbed by ill-health, never seeing that I had got in my own way. I am grateful that I managed to navigate my way out and learn the most amazing life lesson along the way. It's the one that I am passionate about sharing here.

4. *Beth on...*
Your Imagination

The way that we respond to the world is not based on what we actually see, hear, smell, touch and taste, but on our *perception* of what we see, smell, hear, touch or taste.

Perception is defined as recognising sensory information and then analysing and responding to it. The second two parts of this – the analysis and the response – involve using our imagination. It is why the same audition could seem perfectly fine on a good day and unimaginably stressful if it comes after missing the train, going to the wrong address or leaving your phone at home.

Our stress and disturbance does not come from the situation or event, but from the way that we respond to this situation. As we saw in action in the last chapter, there is almost nothing more important to our mental and emotional health than our imagination.

We also know that there are real and lasting benefits to mental health and wellbeing for those who actively build imagination and creativity into our daily lives. Our imagination does not sit in one place in the brain, but is spread out across many; largely it is centred in the neocortex. Science has now shown that there are strong benefits to building neural pathways that connect the neocortex with the prefrontal cortex, the higher-thinking brain. In other words, to use our creativity.

It is something that those of us who have used the creative therapies have always known to be the truth. But now the science is there to back it up. Performers, along with artists of all description, are, of course, in a very strong position to utilise and to build these pathways. This chapter encourages you to use the imaginative skills and techniques you use in your work as a performer, across the range of activities in your daily lives; in fact, to rewire your brain so that this is your natural way of thinking.

The Importance of Imagination

When we were looking at the stress response, we said that our 'fight or flight' instinct kicks in when there is danger or *perceived* danger. The fact that the brain does not distinguish between a situation of real danger and one that we only perceive to be threatening, means that we can use our imagination in a host of ways to help us towards positive mental health and more effective performance.

Of course, if we are imagining something negative then the opposite is also true. As performers we might be asked to create a dark or depressed character or imagine a wholly unsavoury social environment – if we are playing Hamlet or Hedda Gabler, for example. It is essential that awareness of what is going on in our brain and body is raised and protocols built in, so that the damaging effects of this can be curtailed. It is vital that we have exercises that we can do after a performance to take ourselves away from these imagined emotions to release the points of tension that these characters have held. We will revisit this towards the end of this chapter.

The fact that the brain does not distinguish between real and imagined experience is what lies behind the placebo effect, when a person's physical or mental health appears to improve after taking a placebo or 'dummy' treatment. To a very large extent, our brain delivers what we *expect* to feel. In tests throughout the UK and the Western world, placebo drugs currently prove to be between 40% and 72% as effective as the real thing.[1] If this does not show the power of the imagination, then nothing does.

Many of us will have seen this in practice in our creative lives and known it as 'Doctor Theatre'! I have witnessed people move from being physically sick in the wings to stepping onstage to give an outstanding performance. I once saw a performer break fingers during a fight sequence onstage, and not know they had done so until the curtain call.

Of course, it also works in the opposite direction. It is unlikely that many performers will have 'thrown a sickie'[2] (unless perhaps it was while doing casual work between jobs). But it is very common for those who do feign an illness to avoid work or another responsibility, that once they have stated the same excuse twice or three times, they will start to feel pretty unwell!

The Power of Creativity

Creativity is the outward expression of imagination. As performers your imagination and creativity are, of course, your most essential tools. This is likely to be something that you have been aware of since you took your first tentative steps towards the stage. And, of course, it is not just the imagination that you use in the development of your character in rehearsal.

You are constantly creating. It is one of the hardest yet most rewarding things about a life in the performing arts. If you are in a run of a play for six months you still need to create it new, fresh and different, every night. If you do not, then you are simply recreating, working on autopilot, and the audience will know it. And, more importantly, so will you! Recreating provides very few of the chemical rewards that come from creating, which is one of the many reasons that mental health can suffer during a long run of a play.

People we work with who aren't performers often tell us that they are not in any way creative, but actually creativity and imaginative thinking are at the heart of all learning and all human development. A good teacher will evoke your imagination when imparting new information, ensuring that you 'possess' it and make it your own, increasing the likelihood of retention. And creativity is the bridge to innovation. You cannot invent something without imagining it first.

We are creative beings, all of us, and we negotiate every part of our daily lives by imagining. We make decisions by imagining potential futures, and we judge safety and danger through the employment of imagination. We use our imagination to read the emotions of other people, both in everyday life and in performance. That is what makes us voraciously consume TV, film and theatre. It is imagination that engages us in any story or situation, in daily life or in art. We use our imagination to identify with a character's emotions and situation; we decide how we would feel if it were happening to us.

The definition of creativity that always rings true to me is the phrase that Walt Disney coined – 'Imagineering' – which embodies the composite qualities of imagining and engineering. I have always felt that this is the way that the world exists and moves forward. We can break it down into stages – responding analytically, experiencing an emotion, developing an original response, and then implementing it.

A recent study defined some of the qualities that creative people demonstrate. It is certainly an interesting list and one that I think many performers will feel aligned to. It states that:

> Creative people are energetic but focused. They are smart but retain their sense of wonder and an ability to look at the world with fresh eyes. They are playful yet disciplined. And they are persistent. They are realistic dreamers, coming up with imaginative solutions to real-life problems. They interact well with other people, taking ideas from them, and then retreat to isolation to explore them.[3]

And, just as important to remember, the study says that creative people are open and sensitive and therefore vulnerable, prone to mood swings and mental ill-health. I would say, however, that this does not have to be the case. By employing the combined techniques of cognitive behavioural therapy and mindfulness as outlined in this book, it is possible to retain the sensitivity while increasing psychological resilience.

Creativity and Healing

There is a strongly evidenced link between creativity and healing, with a range of creative therapies currently used in the treatment of depression, anxiety and psychosis. The techniques of mindful meditation, of employing an imaginative process, are also widely used in a system of pain management for conditions as wide-ranging as arthritis and cancer. For more details of this you may want to look at the amazing work and research of Dr Jon Kabat-Zinn, who founded the Stress Reduction Clinic and the Center for Mindfulness in Medicine, Healthcare and Society.[4]

Drama therapy has been shown to be hugely successful in schools, hospitals, mental health clinics, community centres and in prisons, perhaps the space in which it is most obviously demonstrates how beneficial and profound a change in thinking can be. In drama therapy, participants work creatively to explore truths about themselves, to understand recurring images, to look at unhealthy patterns of behaviour, to identify triggers and to come to terms with difficult situations. Does all this sound familiar? For many actors it is precisely the process that you will commonly use to analyse, rehearse, prepare and perform a character.

As a creative performer you are in a position of real advantage to use these strategies and techniques from drama therapy as part of your regular plan to develop, manage and maintain your emotional health. Some of the most common exercises and role-plays used in drama therapy include the following:

Naming

Identifying and naming people who have the power to make you feel uncomfortable, irritated or angry, then creating role-play situations in which using the name can take the sting out of difficult past situations. This works because we instinctively avoid using the name of a person who has upset or hurt us – but that gives, in our mind, power to the name and to the person. If you feel you were let down by a producer of a previous project, you could play out a scenario (either one that actually happened, or one from your imagination) and set yourself the goal of naming them ten times through the scene. This can be incredibly empowering, sometimes significantly changing the events of the scene as it plays out.

Role-plays

Role-plays can examine a conflict from a new perspective, either by taking on the role of the other person within the situation or by seeing it through a different worldview. Perhaps there is a director whom you find challenging to work with. You might try playing out a scene that has actually happened or one that you are creating from your imagination. But it could also be effective to take on the role of another actor who finds the director easier than you do to accommodate. Taking on a different worldview in this way is often interesting and effective. A director who is frustrated because their actors do not seem to be recognising their authority could take on the worldview that everyone is equal within the company, and then replay a challenging situation they have encountered from this perspective.

Forum Theatre

This process, pioneered by the Brazilian theatre director Augusto Boal, involves acting out a scene, with an external person stopping it at certain points and adding in conditions and requests, sometimes after an imaginative discussion with onlookers. I have seen this work very effectively to resolve a conflict between two actors who were approaching a devising process from oppositional, equally entrenched positions. They staged a 'chat' about their creative processes and perspectives. At any moment any of the other actors in the company could freeze the 'scene' and hand one of them a note, which the participant had to take on and use constructively. Notes included 'Show interest in her family situation' and 'Ask about the benefits of constant repetition.' At the end of the exercise, both actors said that they had come to realise that their starting points, process and intentions were not as different as they had previously thought.

Playing serious situations with humour can effectively be used to bring down the intensity of negative emotions that are attached to a memory or situation. I remember watching a role-play in which a young woman was confronting a medical practitioner whom she had come to believe had a vendetta against her. She was given the instruction to play some physical comedy, but it never reached that point. The doctor, given a different instruction, one minute into the scene, broke into song. In that instant, the woman was thrown off centre and it was enough for her to begin her journey of re-evaluation.

Imagination in Emotional Health

Your imagination is the tool with which you are able to reframe your thoughts and unlock your potential. But it can do its own damage too. When you start imagining future potential problems – future noise – and conjuring up mental movies hurtling towards worst-case scenarios: that's your imagination working overtime.

The first time you think about an impending audition you may imagine yourself arriving a minute or two late, and in a bit of a fluster. The second time you may imagine yourself stumbling over a line in your monologue. By the time your untamed brain takes you there for the fifth time you may be imagining a scenario whereby you don't turn up at all, or you forget the whole speech, or the director hates you! It is your imagination that will be, to a very great extent, inducing your 'fight or flight' response.

As we have noted, your amygdala will instigate this response when we perceive threat or danger; in other words, when we imagine a situation, such as an audition, to be more threatening than it actually is. In situations where the amygdala becomes hyperactive – in people experiencing post-traumatic stress disorder or acute insomnia, for instance – it is the imagination that will be creating the perception of the entire world as a threatening and dangerous place.

To a lesser extent this will be happening whenever our anxiety has kicked in. If we are worried about an upcoming audition or the end of a contract it is likely that we will be perceiving other aspects of our world as more negative or threatening than they are. Because of the way our brain works it will 'pull' the level of lesser problems up to that of the most serious issue we are facing. It is why, when we are looking at rational thinking, we need to clearly identify the problems that really need our focus and our time.

Of course, the opposite is also true. We can use our imagination constructively to shape what our brain learns from experience. In a therapy situation, imagination is a powerful tool to overcome phobias and post-traumatic stress disorder. It can be used to successfully reshape an emotional response to a memory, and to some extent even reshape the memory itself. It can also be used in exposure therapy, which is where a patient is encouraged repeatedly to imagine the threat in a completely safe environment. In any kind of recovery, we are essentially imagining a future in which we see ourselves as better, and heading for that end result.

The more powerfully we can use our imagination, the more effectively we can solve problems; if things go wrong, the more quickly we can correct the course we are on. We move from negativity to positivity using the ABC method (detailed in the previous chapter) by employing our imagination. And crucially, it is our imagination that enables us to access the meaning that gives value to our life. From this we can visualise the goals that will take us there, and each small step along the way that will allow us to enjoy the journey.

Just as critically, and especially so for those in the creative industries, it is our imagination that allows us to empathise. We are able to walk in another person's shoes, to inhabit another's thoughts and emotions, and from this experience to gain understanding, and channel these into performance. Building psychological resilience depends enormously on enhancing emotional intelligence, and most importantly the development of empathy. It is another advantage enjoyed by those in the performing arts – this is what we do for a living.

Revisit the exercise Expanding Your Empathy in Chapter 1, where we simply visualise a situation from the perspective of another person and then tell the 'story' as if we are them. As we become more practised at it, we are able to bring this from something that we have to do consciously (or even retrospectively), into the present, into the now. We can use our imagination to sense the outcome of a particular decision. Or to find a moment of contact or communion. And when we are giving ourselves entirely to the present moment, it is our imagination that allows us to link the specific instance to the big picture, to see the spider's web of related issues that spin off from any situation, allowing us understanding of context and meaning.

Imagination for Performers

Working as a performer, you will be very familiar with using your imagination as part of your ongoing process. You imagine something, you try it out, you evaluate, you make a few adjustments, and you imagine it again. This isn't something that most people are used to doing, at least not on a conscious basis.

For many, using their imagination to visualise and to empathise can be something that takes a good deal of committed time and practice. But many performers will already have these finely tuned skills. Put simply, it is the detail that counts. Many performers will be familiar with Stanislavskian sense memory exercises, in which you focus on an event, perhaps something important that has happened in the life of your character, and imagine it happening to you in real time.[5] You will therefore be used to imagining all that you can see, smell, hear, touch and taste in exceptional detail.

Performers are likely to be able to empathise better, having the ability to create characters with different belief systems, and a different way of seeing the world. Experiencing a different worldview in this way often results in a more open mindset that allows you to take on new beliefs more easily, including those necessary to gain the most from each and every chapter of this book.

It is also likely that you will be better at creating new neural pathways, because you will be using adaptive behaviour. This is adopting a practice of small but continual change, which results in the brain building neural pathways more quickly and more effectively. You do this as you move from contract to contract, company to company, place to place and role to role. This is almost unheard-of in any other working environment. You will also be using adaptive behaviour and building new pathways every time you add a new character facet to the role you are creating, or try playing the scene in a different way.

You will already be skilled in collaborative practice. Every time you improvise, you are demonstrating the best of mindfulness and adaptive behaviour. You are responding absolutely in the moment, and you are taking on new thinking because you are incorporating the ideas of someone else into your mindset. In many of our performance workshops we start with an exercise that you may already know.

Exercise: Journey Pair

- Try this exercise with a friend; first, decide who is A and who is B.

- Then link arms and tell a story one word each. A begins the story with 'We' – and you only speak as 'we', never as 'I'.

- B continues with, for example, 'crept' as you both make a creeping movement. A may add 'into', B may add 'safety' while you both drop into a hiding position, looking out to check that you really are safe.

There is almost nothing that you can do that will more effectively build new neural pathways, strengthen adaptive behaviour, and bring you into the moment.

The following series of guided meditations and exercises will harness your imagination to move you towards mental and emotional health; they combine creative processes with focused attention, working from a place of rest.

Guided Exercise: Butterflies ◀ᴐ 3

- Sit comfortably and close your eyes. Imagine that you are in a clearing in the forest. It is a beautiful sunny day. Spend a moment looking around you and noticing the colours, the sounds and the smells.

- In the distance you see a kaleidoscope of butterflies coming towards you. As they get closer, notice their beauty, the shape and colour of their wings, and the way they move. They come close to you, just a few feet away, and they begin to circle you.

- Notice that some of the butterflies have entered your body. They move through you and begin to heal you, clearing any blocks. Notice the areas that they are healing, and how this feels.

- Others remain circling you. Observe that they are taking your negative thoughts and feelings onto their wings, and flying away with them.

- The butterflies moving through you finish their work. Take a moment to notice what it feels like to be totally and completely healed.

- All of the butterflies circle you one last time and then hover in front of you, perhaps saying goodbye. You feel a great sense of connection to them, before you watch them fly off into the distance.

- Spend a moment just reflecting on the significance of the experience. And in your own time open your eyes, and come back to the present moment.

Guided Exercise: Foxhole in Your Mind Extended
◀)) 4

We first experienced this exercise in Chapter 2. This time we are going to take it one step further. This time we are going to enter and exit your imagined space by using a personal trigger. Mine is two taps of my right hand on my left shoulder. I know others who use a clap or a raised eyebrow that cannot be detected in meetings!

With practice, this trigger will help you move more quickly into your foxhole – your specific, imagined space that you populate with positive objects and surroundings.

- Close your eyes. Perform your trigger action now to take you in.

- I would like you to imagine a safe and beautiful space. Imagine it in as much detail as you can – objects, colours, sounds, smells. It works best if it is the same place that you imagine each time you do the exercise, so recreate the physical space you imagined when you did the exercise earlier.

- Once you have the space as clearly defined as possible, place yourself inside it, moving round, reacting to what you are experiencing. This time focus strongly on the senses. Know exactly what you can see, smell, hear, touch and taste.

- In your own time, trigger out by performing your trigger action again. Open your eyes and come back to the present moment.

- Make a note of your trigger. Make a note of any changes to your foxhole since the time you last visited, or any changes to the emotions or sensations you experienced.

- This is a space that you can 'visit' whenever you need to 'step away' from a stressful event or situation. The more often you do it, the more quickly it will work.

Guided Exercise: Gratitude for a Special Person
🔊 5

We have explored the concept of gratitude before. Any gratitude exercise should, in fact, involve you actively imagining the object or person that you are grateful for, and, importantly, feeling the gratitude, rather than just reeling off a list.

In this exercise we are concentrating on using gratitude to strengthen and deepen a relationship that is important to you.

- Close your eyes and imagine someone for whom you are sincerely and profoundly grateful. As you do this exercise keep the image clear, while breathing in through the nose and out through the mouth.

- Think about each of these concepts in turn while imagining the person:

  Everything changes when you start really listening to another person.

  Everything changes when you stop being judgemental.

  Everything changes when you start noticing what the person *is* doing, rather than what they aren't.

  Everything changes when you stop taking things personally.

- Make a note of anything you realised about the person, yourself, or the relationship during the exercise.

We all sabotage relationships by being judgemental, and by not appreciating the other person and what they do for us. This is a simple exercise to turn this around.

Once you have mastered it, you can apply it to people with whom you are struggling to have a constructive relationship, perhaps in your personal life, or perhaps a demanding director or fellow actor.

Exercise: Imagination for Conflict Resolution

This exercise works well to reduce conflict that exists in a personal area of your life, or in a professional situation.

- Sit yourself comfortably and close your eyes. Select a person with whom you have a conflicted relationship.

- Think of a situation between you and this person that you know needs to be resolved. Perhaps it is something you know you need to ask, but have been putting off. Or something you weren't happy about, and know needs to be spoken about, so that it doesn't happen again.

- Imagine exactly where this 'conversation' is taking place, and where each of you are sitting or standing. And now play the scene through in your imagination. For example, you may imagine yourself asking the director of your current show why the notes they gave you were, or seemed, more personal than was necessary. Imagine their reply and really listen to it, trying to understand their reasoning and point of view. Continue the conversation in your mind until you feel that a resolution has been reached. It should not last more than three minutes.

- After the scene open your eyes and think rationally about how it went. Could it have gone better for you? If so, replay it, tweaking the responses to what you are saying, so that it becomes more positive. Notice how differently you have to behave in order to make this happen.

- Repeat the scene up to five times, each time acknowledging the different input from you and the changing results.

You cannot, of course, make another person behave in the way that you want. But it is interesting that often after doing this exercise, resolutions in the real world are easier to achieve than expected. Perhaps you ask your questions in a less confrontational way and are more prepared to listen or be patient. Even if it does not lead to a resolution of the conflict in 'real life', it is likely to leave you less distressed or disturbed by it, because you know that you have done all that you can.

Exercise: Imagination for Overcoming the Inner Critic 📖 17

The whole concept of self-image is based around imagination. We are literally hypnotised by our self-image, either negative or positive; in other words, whatever we imagine ourselves to be, we are. And this self-image determines the way we see the world, and everything that happens to us and around us.

- Next time that you notice negative self-talk creeping in, make a note of it.

- Then imagine a critic standing behind you speaking these negative thoughts to you.

- If you are doubting the way you are playing a character or a scene, for example, give 'voice' to this. Imagine the critic saying, 'Your emotional breakdown in Scene Two is crap.' It is important that you use the spiteful, non-sophisticated language that is the basis of so many of our automatic negative thoughts. If the critic was saying 'Your emotional journey through Scene Two is not as credible as it could be', you probably wouldn't be able to counter it so vigorously.

- Now turn and confront this outrageous critic, countering each and every statement. If someone else were attacking you in this way, what would you say? Make a note of the powerful statements that you use.

- After the exercise, commit your counter-attack to memory, so that you can use it the next time the negative self-talk creeps in.

We know that creativity is an integral part of good mental health, and an important part of cognitive functioning. For example, we know how highly creativity is rated by the human brain; when we have a moment of creative insight then our brain and autonomic nervous system shut down, just for a nanosecond. All focus goes to the moment of insight. Isn't that amazing?

We also know that the more moments of focused attention we are able to cultivate, the more moments of creative insight we will have as a result. Many techniques throughout this book will help you to experience, and maintain, focused attention. We also know that imaginative and creative thought comes most easily in the relaxed but alert state that is induced by mindfulness. Perhaps it can be summed up by the feeling of trusting, rather than trying too hard.

Key is our understanding that adopting a practice of adaptive behaviour will mean that we are more likely to continually think, move and create outside the box. As performers, this is pure gold. Related to this is our understanding that because of the way that neuroplasticity works, our brain will always take the route of least resistance. Once we know this, we are able to guide it more easily in another direction. Try this following exercise based on the Laban Kinesphere.

Exercise: The Kinesphere

- Stand with your feet shoulder-width apart, relax for a moment, and then close your eyes.

- You are now going to spend one minute keeping your feet flat on the floor, but moving as far as you can in every direction, so that you use your hands to define your kinesphere, the space that you are able to reach and inhabit from your grounded position. Make sure you lean forwards and backwards, and move out to each side at high levels and low.

- As you do so, be aware of the space that you are creating and taking up. Also be aware of the lines you are making as you create this space, the most frequent moves, and the energy qualities that you consistently use. Perhaps make a few basic energy observations: do you mainly move low or high, light or heavy, focused or dissipated, jerky or flowing, bound or free? Now start to become aware of the areas that you have not moved towards, the lines you have not taken, the energy qualities that you have not used. Try to use these directions and own those spaces.

- After the exercise, consider the lines and energy qualities that you instinctively used, and those that you did not.

The point of this exercise is that when we are, for example, building a physical character, we like to think that we are stepping away from the lines and energy qualities that are us, and taking up those of the character that we are building. However, because of the way that neuroplasticity works we are likely to be moving in particular directions and taking up particular spaces rather than others. We will, whether we realise it or not, be following habitual patterns that belong to us rather than the character we are creating.

I always point out, for example, that my movement going forwards and down are pretty good for my age. I am able to put my palms flat on the floor. However, when I move backwards or diagonally I am suddenly much less supple! If I don't create a character consciously, I will build my habitual movements into my performance without even realising that they are mine. Once you understand this concept, you will be able to step to the side of your path of least resistance more often, and begin to be truly original in the way that you create. You can become one of the rare and wonderful actors that are able to step away from themselves, and be unrecognisably different and innovative in every role you take on.

Imagination and Memory

Since imagination and memory are intrinsically linked, we can use the former to improve the latter! This is something that we have found particularly important with older performers, who have become less confident in learning and remembering lines.

Line-learning and retention can be helped by imagining an image or a movement to go with the line of text that we wish to remember. Many performers will already be doing this instinctively. It is why it is so much harder to remember lines before a scene has been blocked, because that process reinforces line retention with muscle memory, spatial awareness and emotional recall. And, again, developing adaptive behaviour and getting better at building new neural pathways will also strengthen memory retention.

Try to commit to using your imagination in your everyday life as much as you do in the life that you inhabit as a performer. One easy way is applying a basic 'What if?' to every situation you encounter, much like Stanislavsky's 'Magic If' that we apply onstage.

We all understand the power of imagining a condition of the scene, to change the context and consequences in any given situation. If we do an improvisation in which we are simply shopping in the supermarket, and apply the first 'What if?' as imagining we have just found out that someone close to us is seriously ill, and the second 'What if?' as imagining we have just found out that we have won the lottery, we know how profoundly the shopping routine would change! And not just our shopping habits, but our thoughts, emotions and energy. We can apply this to our everyday life to engage our imagination, to induce positivity, and to help change our perception of unpleasant or unhelpful events.

What if the cast member who has just been offhand with you had an argument with their partner this morning? What if the missed call from your agent that you won't be able to return until lunchtime was an audition with the RSC? It is simply a way of ensuring that you are feeling and acting like the shopper who has won the lottery a little more often in your life.

Imagination and the Stretch Zone

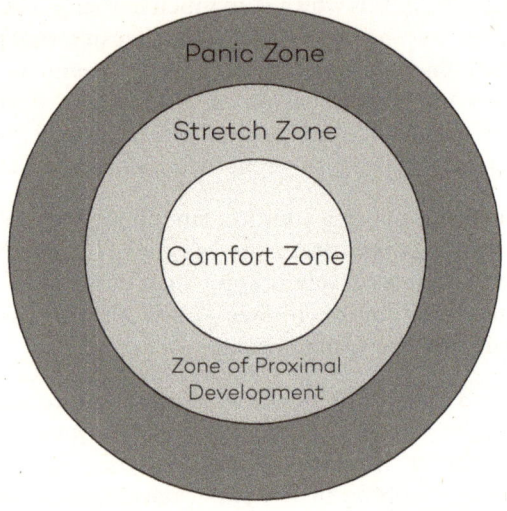

We have three zones in which we work. Imagine this as three concentric circles around you. Closest to us is the Comfort Zone, where everything is safe, easy and familiar, just the way we like it. Beyond this is the Zone of Proximal Development, or Stretch Zone. It is called the Stretch Zone because we want to expand it, stretch it, as much as we can. Finally, comes the Panic Zone, which is too overwhelming, stressful and scary.

The reason we want to expand the Stretch Zone is because it is the only space in which new neural pathways can be made. In order to learn and to create we must step out of the Comfort Zone, and step back from the Panic Zone, as needed.

Exercise: Stretch Zone 📖 18

- Try to recall a situation where you stepped outside of your Comfort Zone. Connect, for a moment, with how that felt. Make a note of this. Now do the same for a time when you have successfully pulled yourself back from the Panic Zone. Make a note of this.

- Now make a note of something impending, for which you know you will have to step outside your Comfort Zone to achieve the best results. We can do this by creating conditions in which we can push ourselves just slightly off centre.

- In whatever it is that you're attempting to do, place on it an imaginary condition that forces you to take a risk, to step out of the Comfort Zone and into the Stretch Zone. For example, imagine that a casting director who loves highly charged emotional performances is in the audience watching you. Or imagine that the agent you most want to take you on has recommended you for this audition. And enjoy it!

Conclusion

To conclude this chapter on using your imagination, I would like to talk about something that might be seen as a negative, but that I see as the most important reason performers use their imagination in a positive way, to move them towards real emotional health.

You may have realised that, as someone with an active and exercised imagination, you have real power to drive yourself towards the positive, but it also means you have the potential to do the opposite. It is likely that the negative mental movies that you create, and the imagery of your worst-case scenarios, will be more compelling and more convincing than those constructed by people less used to being creative. You are skilled at convincing others with the pictures, characters, relationships and situations you imagine, but of course you are using the same skills when you imagine a dreadful audition or the rent that can't be paid. It is essential therefore that you learn to use your imagination in a positive way.

In addition to all the specific reasons related to mental and emotional health explored in this chapter, you will know something that is equally true and important. Imagination makes our world more vibrant and makes us feel more alive. It is the quintessential ingredient to unlocking the most vital and vibrant you.

5. *Beth on...*
Your Body

The old argument that raged for centuries was 'Are we a body with a mind, or a mind with a body?' Descartes with his famous 'I think therefore I am' came firmly down on the side of a mind with a body. But where in this mind/body separation is the existence of a spirit or soul?

Ask Westerners where the mind is and they will often point to their head, as that's where they think mindfulness operates, but anyone who has undertaken any mindfulness will know that it is a whole-body practice.

Ancient Buddhist philosophers have always understood the integral mind/body relationship. Thanks to neuroscience we now know that this is true. The harmonious coexistence of mind and body is what underpins consciousness.

In fact, the extent to which the mind and body are linked goes much further than this. We know now that given repeated trauma (or perceived trauma), the amygdala becomes metabolically reactive and can increase to double the usual size.[1] We know that every positive relational experience we have with any other person changes not just the function but also the composition of both our brain and theirs.

And, of course, the opposite is also true. Every negative relational experience – every time we criticise, complain and judge – negatively impacts both our brain and that of the other person. We have not yet come to terms with the responsibility that this places on us as a species. We are surely headed towards a world in which we will only see 'health' rather than considering mental and physical health as separate entities. This is to be welcomed as it will, in all likelihood, reduce the stigma around mental (ill-) health that stubbornly persists.

The subject of this book is emotional health – and this *must* encompass both brain and body. Our emotions are induced by chemicals that are instigated by thoughts, positive or negative. Every emotion we feel is manifested in the body. It is this expression of emotion that we, as performers, reveal to an audience.

It is accepted wisdom now that physical exercise is essential for good mental health. Any exercise plan will deliver benefits to your emotional health and boost a general sense of wellbeing, although we would recommend one that does not focus on the way that you look.

One of the very best creative therapies for boosting mental health and wellbeing is dance. This is because it combines imagination with sensory and auditory stimuli and responses, as well as physical movement and expression. In fact, I recommend that if you find a time when you're unable to focus on any exercise outlined in this book, you simply put on your favourite piece of music – and dance!

Exercise is also important for good sleep, which is itself essential for good mental and emotional health. Sleep scientists tell us that 150 minutes of exercise a week can result in a 65% improvement in sleep for those experiencing insomnia. We know now that of the 'Health Trinity' – exercise, nutrition and sleep – it is sleep that is by far the most important of the three.

The links between mind and body are, of course, bidirectional. In other words, the state of mind impacts the body and the state of body impacts the mind. One of the most revealing examples of this is the role that mental training plays in the healing process. It has been shown that even with patients living with cancer, cultivating and maintaining a positive mindset will deliver a more positive prognosis. And, of course, you have heard about the placebo effect in the chapter on imagination. So, we must ask ourselves: if the way we *think* can have this great an impact on the way the body *feels* and *heals*, what else can it do?

We believe that good emotional health is developed by working holistically on the whole person: the body as well as the mind. We can use our new thinking to make us feel comfortable with the way our bodies look and move and function. And we must also use our bodies to help us on the journey towards mental and emotional health.

We are electrochemical organisms, and every change that occurs in our brain ripples through an almost infinite number of places in our body. If we are looking to maximise the good feelings and the good emotions, then we should not ignore the joy that can come from the physical sensations of touch and movement. Performers will be very used to the physical pleasure that comes through performance, the feeling of oneness with others as we enter the creative 'dance'.

In all areas of life, our bodies are an integral part of the way that we connect with other people. A great deal of pleasure can come from simple touch, a hug or sitting close to somebody else, where the happiness chemical oxytocin is released through the body, and the amount that this can contribute to good mental and emotional health cannot be underestimated. It is one of the factors that plays heavily in the detrimental effects of social isolation. You may be aware that it is now believed that loneliness takes more lives than smoking.

Here I am going to detail a range of exercises that fuse body and mind for performers used to working in this way, and give some examples of when to use them.

Guided Exercise: Finding the Gaps Between Breaths 🔊 6

- Sit comfortably with your feet flat on the floor and your spine straight.

- Close your eyes and focus on your breath without trying to change it. Notice which parts of your body move as you breathe. Notice your natural rhythm.

- After a minute, notice the small gaps between the in-breath and the out-breath.

- After a further minute, begin to 'rest' in each of these gaps, without extending them. Do this for one minute.

We are sometimes asked if 'resting' is relaxing into the gaps between the breaths. It is this, yes, but when you become practised, it is more than that. It is almost as though your world expands, the sense that the 'gap' is going on forever, even though the natural rhythm you identified has not changed. And it can be a new kind of 'rest', an absolute calm, absolute peace, without the giving-up of energy. Some people report an overwhelming sense of connection, finding in these gaps a bridge between the internal and the external world.

It is a hugely effective exercise. I clearly remember the moment when I first recognised that I was using it. I was challenged in a confrontational way by the director of a venue. I was aware of the space, the 'moment in time', between their outburst and my reaction to it. I was able to 'rest' for the briefest moment in a space that allowed me to frame a rational response.

Focusing on the breath will, of course, always bring you back to the present moment. We can only breathe in the now. But actually this is true of any of our senses. You can only see, smell, hear, touch and taste in the present moment. As a performer you are likely to be aware of which senses you most rely on. You may also be aware of those that are weaker, that you wish to develop. Choose the exercises from this chapter and throughout the book that work best for you – although I would also encourage you to step outside of your Comfort Zone and use a new exercise from time to time.

In school we are taught that we have five senses – sight, smell, sound, touch and taste. In fact, there are a lot more. Neurologists typically work with between nine and twenty-one. These include the perception of pressure, vibration, heat and pain. They also include the sense of balance and proprioception, the brain's knowledge of the relative position of body parts. This sense is, of course, key to performers, and working kinaesthetically is something that you will be very used to doing.

Guided Exercise: Back to Centre 🔊 7

This exercise uses the mind and proprioception: your body's ability to sense movement, action, posture and location. This is the solo version of the exercise, but it can be done just as well in pairs.

- Stand with your feet shoulder-width apart in a comfortable and centered position.

- Release any tension in your shoulders while keeping your spine straight. Make sure that your head is balanced, and close your eyes.

- First be aware of the sensation of being entirely centred and balanced. Focus in on this feeling as deeply as you can. Now you are going to move each body part singly, while keeping your feet flat on the floor and still.

- Take all your focus to the part of your body that is moving. If, for example, your arms swing forwards, take all your focus and attention to the movement of your arm. As each part of your body comes back to the neutral starting position, be aware again of that feeling of being fully centred before you move the next part of your body. As with any mindfulness exercise, if any other thoughts come into your mind just gently let them drift away and bring your attention back to the part of your body that you are moving.

- If you are doing this exercise in pairs then A stands in neutral with their eyes closed. B stands behind them and moves each part of A's body, allowing them to come back to centre each time.

- You may find that the exercise helps you to locate any points of tension that you are holding. Make a note of these. The next time you do the exercise, focus on these, and give time to allow these tense areas to 'soften'.

This is a great exercise to do when you feel ungrounded, or to hone mind/body coordination just before an audition or performance.

The Mind/Body Link in Performance

Awareness of our body can certainly help us to be more aware of the emotions that we are feeling and the physical manifestations of these. Performers are already used to identifying and using these manifestations onstage. For example, fear can make us run, or it can root us to the spot; it can take our breath away; give us a cold, icy feeling or hot, prickly sensation.

Increased awareness can also help us to recognise the physiological signs of an approaching or 'arising' emotion. Once you start to recognise the physical signs of, say, anger or fear, you can begin to head them off before they engulf you.

Throughout this book we describe the importance of building new neural pathways. As you know, whenever we think or do something new, we build a new neural pathway, and whatever we think about the most becomes our strongest pathway, which our brain will use as the route of least resistance. Our bodies, our actions and our movements are an integral part of this.

One of the things that becomes harder as we head into our later years is that, as movement becomes more challenging, we can only rely on our thinking to build these new neural pathways. It is movement, the 'doing', that allows the process of building new neural pathways to be more expansive. A pathway is only new if it is something we have not thought before, but if we can add a different action or movement to it, then the connection becomes new. For example, the Journey Pair Exercise (described in Chapter 4) is about listening and about being in the moment, and that could be done sitting on chairs just telling the story. By moving it around, by physicalising it, you are also building new neural pathways that are connecting the words, concepts and movements.

When you work using your whole body, it becomes an experience. Anything that is experienced will stay in your imagination and in your memory in a much more powerful way. It is why experiential learning – the process of learning by *doing* – is such a powerful tool. We know that memory sits not just in one place but in many, and is coloured by perception every time we use the process of recall. Memory that encompasses action remains more vivid and is easier to recall.

Too often when we feel something – whether this is physical or emotional – we ignore it, indulge it or fight it. But we need to learn to accept it, to explore it rationally and to understand why it is there. And if necessary to move through it, and then to move on. Emotions and physical sensations, including pain, are there for a reason; they are there to warn us that things may not be as good as they could be, and it is time for us to take whatever action needs to be taken.

Sharpening and tightening the way we focus helps to improve the way we select and express our character's intentions when we are performing. This may not, at first consideration, seem relevant to physical performance, but of course it is. Some years ago, I did a performance of a play based on the story of Hercules, with a profoundly disabled cast. The role of the Ferryman who takes Hercules across the River Styx was played by a young actor I will call Sheldon. He was in a wheelchair and only had limited movement in his right arm. He was visually impaired but was able to see one shade that sat on the colour spectrum between white and lilac.

Our stage manager built a boat with a sail that opened on a button press. Sheldon took his place on the boat and with an enormous effort reached out his right arm and a forty-foot sail, in exactly the right shade between white and lilac, filled the stage. I have never in my life seen a performance more physical, or one where the physicality had a more profound effect on the audience. It was the level of focus and intention. Just that.

There is a synergy between aspects of the programme of change set out in this book and the techniques you will already be using as a performer. Three of the most important are:

Awareness

Performers very often have a high level of awareness of their body and physicality. You will be conscious of the way your body feels, moves and responds. Alongside this, there will be a high level of awareness of thoughts, emotions and relative space, which we have referenced often. Gaining and maintaining awareness is a key part of the processes employed in this book.

Gut instinct

Almost all creative people will count instinct as one of the skills they rely upon. Many performers go as far as describing a physical sensation that they connect to instinct, usually located around the stomach. I remember being thrilled when the gut instinct I have always valued so highly was found to have a basis in science. The enteric nervous system (ENS) in our gut is a hub of intelligence, having roughly the same number of neurons as the brain of a dog.[2] This second brain can react without consulting or communicating with our first brain, so all the sayings that we have always used in the creative world – 'gut instinct', 'gut reaction', 'gut-wrenching' – bear this out. The relationship between gut and brain also means that almost anything that is good for your brain is also good for your gut, and therefore your physical health.

Stillness

Performers are used to finding and inhabiting moments of stillness, an important concept in mindfulness. For many non-performers, stillness is equated with an exhausted 'slumping', the equivalent in acting terms of energy being given up to the chair or the floor. In mindfulness practice we aim for an alert but relaxed state, which is akin to the energy-held state we use onstage. We are absolutely still, but containing our energy within us rather than giving it up, ready to move when required.

Here are two exercises that suit performers well, as they employ your body, mind and imagination.

Exercise: Mindful Walking 📖 19

- Take a walk in nature – for example, in a park, in the countryside, or by the coast.

- Notice the feeling of your feet on the ground. Notice the movement of each part of your body as you step. Notice your weight as it moves through your feet and works upwards. Notice how each part of your body is connected. Notice whether the rhythm of your steps corresponds to the rhythm of your breath. Write down five things that you noticed.

- Notice the natural world around you in detail. Use all your senses. Bring your focused attention to a single leaf or stone, or to the smell of a flower or the sound of a bird. Write down five things that you noticed.

- Now bring the two together so that you are aware of both your internal and external world.

As a performer, you will most likely be skilled in reading the body language of others. We know that our brain interprets our own body language in exactly the same way, delivering up the appropriate chemicals and emotions – and, as you know, every emotion is induced by a chemical or compound of chemicals released through the body. By changing negative to positive thinking, we can change the chemicals that are released, resulting in a more positive emotional state. We can do exactly the same thing by changing the way we hold our body, stand and move. Groundbreaking studies proving this were conducted by Amy Cuddy and Dana Carney, who coined the term 'Power Poses'.[3]

Exercise: Power Poses

- Stand in an open, 'high status' position, perhaps with your arms open and stretched upwards. Remain in this position for ninety seconds. Your brain will read this as a positive state and will release adrenalin and testosterone that will make you feel powerful and confident.

- Next, stand in a closed, 'low status' position, perhaps hunched over with your head down, for ninety seconds. Your brain will read this as a negative state, and will release the stress hormone cortisol that we have mentioned before.

- Finish the exercise by standing once again in the powerful position. Try to keep this posture, or the memory of it, and the chemicals and emotions it releases, throughout your daily life.

When I first found out about Power Poses I determined that when I next held auditions I would go and have a look in the waiting room. Almost every actor that I was about to audition was sitting hunched over in a chair in the kind of pose that depicts anxiety and low status. Almost all of them would've been shooting their body through with hormones that would not help them once they came into the audition. But as actors we all have the skills to change this quickly and effectively, building an open physicality that allows the flow of positive hormones into our everyday lives.

Mindfulness and Your Body

By improving your ability, through mindfulness, to be in the moment, you will increase your creative insight, your ability to visualise and imagine, and your resilience. Every moment of active awareness offers the possibility of realising a truth. In essence, perhaps, this is what creative insight is. A sharpened sensory focus will also help you to be more consistently 'present' and lend vibrancy to your expression in performance.

Understanding *how* our emotions work helps us to manage these emotions. You can apply this not only to control your own emotions, but those of the characters you inhabit. For example, you know what is happening to the brain and body of your character when they are pushed into 'fight or flight' mode. Think for a moment how commonly this occurs in plays! You know how to move a character from an unhealthy negative emotion to a healthy negative emotion, if that is useful to their journey through the play. And increased levels of emotional intelligence and empathy will evolve a better understanding of the relationship between your character and the other characters in the play.

Understanding your body and its link to your emotions can also help you to let go of these when you need to, at the end of a rehearsal or performance. This next exercise can stop you taking the character's emotions into your own outside life.

Exercise: Releasing Emotions

- Stand with your feet shoulder-width apart. Close your eyes.

- Visualise the emotion that you wish to release as located in your stomach, chest, throat or wherever feels right to you. Some people like to imagine the emotion as a liquid or a colour. Notice any physical effects emanating from the emotion, but keep it in your body. Don't let any automatic negative thoughts into your mind.

- For a moment, work to 'accept' the emotion, and then gently let it go from wherever you are holding it. Feel it draining down through your legs and out through the soles of your feet into the floor beneath you.

- Finally, notice the difference in the way your body feels once free of this emotion.

Exercise: Limiting Beliefs

Developing your emotional health through the exercises in this book will remove the limiting beliefs that you have about your physical performance.

These states of mind, or of belief, will be restricting you in some way; things like 'I'm not good enough', 'I'll never be successful', 'I'm too old/young/tall/short...' All perfectly natural – and all signs of your brain's desire to protect you from pain in the future – but limiting and restricting you in every way from achieving what you can.

- If you have not identified your limiting beliefs yet, then take a moment to think about them now.

- And then try challenging them in the way that you have been shown in Chapter 3 by using the ABC method, and reframing any demands to preferences. (The next exercise will also help to tackle these limiting beliefs.)

Exercise: The Physical Performer

- Start by recalling the most exciting physical performance that you have seen. I have three clear choices when I am doing this exercise: Steven Berkoff in *Metamorphosis*, Mark Rylance as Ariel in *The Tempest*, and Antony Sher as a very physical *Richard III* on crutches.

- When you have chosen the physical performance you most remember, spend two minutes recalling it in as much detail as you can. How did the performer hold themselves, breathe and move? How did their physicality change through the play? What was it that took your breath away?

- The second stage of the exercise is to visualise yourself undertaking the same performance and fulfilling it physically in exactly the same way. Choose a specific one-minute segment of the performance that you are going to visualise. In this visualisation, notice the way your body is moving, its physical shape, the energy qualities.

- The third stage is to find a space and actively physicalise this one-minute sequence, being led by the detail that you have imagined, fully embodying all that you have admired. Trust your body and your intuition.

- And finally, select a one-minute segment of the play you are currently working on, auditioning for, have recently worked on, or would like to be working on, and repeat stages two and three detailed above – at first visualising, and then physicalising the character – thereby extending their physical remit and potential.

Conclusion

As both people and performers, we must choose to look after our bodies, to understand the relationship between mind, body and emotions, and to commit to doing the best that we can for each part of this vitally important, interdependent triumvirate.

We must accept the way that our body changes, over time and even from moment to moment. We spend so much time battling, in our mind, the injuries that we sustain rather than accepting them, which would in turn facilitate a faster recovery.

Remember that accepting where we are today is not the same as resigning ourselves to being in that same place tomorrow. And for many performers it is a real concern that we are not accepting the ageing process as well as we could. We have spoken with a number of actors who believe that getting older has reduced the possibility of work. This relates both to the way they look and move, and, of course, to the way that they feel, and the way that they are seen by the profession.

In establishing a positive mindset, I believe that it is vitally important that we do not gossip, do not complain and do not condemn. This includes the way that so many of us complain about our bodies, and sometimes about the bodies of other people. These days I only allow myself to complain about things if I am doing all that I can to change them. There are certainly things within the industry that we can all do to change the way that the ageing process disadvantages performers, especially women. Alongside that, we must accept that we age. As a bottom line, getting older is a privilege that not everybody has.

It is very important to establish a clear pattern of letting-go and relaxing at the end of our working day. As a director working with disabled actors and those with mental health issues, I have to put in as many protective protocols as possible. We devise a character warm-up to get the actors into character, an eight-move sequence based around the personal and energy qualities of the character, so that they become acutely aware of the points of tension that their character carries. We always ensure that we let go of these points of tension at the end of every rehearsal, by doing the sequence again, this time focusing on letting go of the tension, holding for a minute, and then moving to the sides with their own energy and physical shape.

I understand the implications of a brain that does not distinguish between real and imagined experience, and I now believe that it is important to go further. If we are playing characters who demonstrate a negative or perhaps aggressive pattern of thinking or physical action, then at the end of the rehearsal we must consciously replace that negative with a positive before leaving the rehearsal room and heading home. We visualise a collective positive goal, celebrate the achievements of each person during the session, or simply put some music on and have a dance!

6. *Andy on...*
Your Emotions

As a performer, you'll be able to create and express emotions. But it's one thing to be able to control emotions in your craft, and a completely different thing to manage them offstage in order to heighten your emotional intelligence and establish emotional control. If one led automatically to the other, then all actors would be the most stable people on earth – and as we all know, that simply isn't the case. Actors are as vulnerable as anyone else. We are all human.

In this chapter we'll be looking more closely at emotions, in order to identify those that trip us up and cause us to get in our own way. By now you are aware that emotions, both positive and negative, are induced by chemicals being released through the body. Now let's look a little deeper.

Emotions and the ABC Model

In Chapter 3 we looked at the ABC model, which enables the process of self-discovery, awareness and realisation. I used the example of my early life, and we used it to formulate my paralysing anxiety, identifying and reframing my unhelpful, rigid and self-sabotaging beliefs. Here's a reminder of the ABC model:

A = Activating event/Adversity
B = Beliefs
C = Consequences (Emotional, Behavioural, Physiological)

Remember, it's not the *situation* (the thing that happens) that leads to our *response*, but the *beliefs* (attitudes, expectations and personal rules) we hold about the situation. In this section I'm going to explain more about how this works.

As a performer, you'll be aware of the wide range of emotions and feelings that exist, and you understand and harness that knowledge in order to act authentically, from the heart. Your experience as an actor affords you a level of emotional insight that most non-performers simply don't possess.

When applying the process of Rational Emotive Behavioural Therapy (REBT),[1] a therapist or coach diligently explores issues with their client. Through skilled questioning and guided discovery, together they will steadily piece together the core of particular issues or challenges. The process will enable the client to identify underlying unhealthy negative emotions that contribute to their disturbance.

This process of discovery can be complex because, without the appropriate knowledge, we tend to confuse feelings and emotions. Feelings are experienced consciously, whilst emotions can manifest both consciously and unconsciously. This is why people can spend years not understanding their true emotions – and because of this, they can struggle for a lifetime.

Emotional literacy can be all the more challenging because we may experience a range of emotions in a situation. If we're anxious, we may also feel angry with ourselves for reacting in that way, accompanied by a sense of guilt that we are letting others down. It can be an emotional minefield.

The emotional confusion results in our getting in our own way. It feels far too difficult to untangle, so we live with troublesome situations and accept the outcomes – such as stress, unhappiness and low contentment – as the price of being who we are. This is why so many people find great benefit from therapy and coaching. It's also why I became fascinated by REBT, appreciating that the ABC model supports better mental health by allowing us to tackle psychological disturbance. Emotional understanding is the next step in the ABC journey.

Here's a quick reminder of my story, more fully described in Chapter 3. I experienced what I now understand to be severe anxiety linked broadly to my fear of performing. My ABC model formulation looked like this:

A = Activating event/Adversity:
'I forget my lines and feel sick.'

B = Beliefs:
'I *must not* forget my lines. I *must not* let people down. I *must not* be sick.'
'It would be *awful* if the cast saw through my lack of experience.'
'I *cannot stand* the prospect of being seen as incompetent.'

C = Consequences:
Emotion: 'I feel anxiety.'
Behaviour: 'I become self-protective, quiet and withdrawn and want to run away.'
Physiology: 'I feel sick and experience sweating, a dry mouth, a pounding heart and memory lapses.'

Let's look at another example:

A = Activating event/Adversity:
'My friend from drama school has posted on Instagram that they're just starting work on a new TV series.'

B = Beliefs:
'I must be useless because I'm not getting any castings.'
'I can't stand that I'm not working whilst everyone else seems to be busy.'

C = Consequences:
Emotion: 'I feel envy, shame, depression, anxiety.'
Behaviour: 'I will withdraw from social media. I will stop seeing my friends. I will call my agent and demand to be taken more seriously. I will give up the business.'

You'll notice that one of the emotional consequences of the beliefs outlined here is anxiety. This is what Rational Emotive Behavioural Therapy refers to as an 'unhealthy negative emotion'. That should make sense, as we would certainly regard that form of anxiety as unhealthy and negative.

Albert Ellis, one of the founding fathers of modern Cognitive Behavioural Therapy, understood the dilemma of emotional confusion.[2] Is it possible to support someone experiencing psychological disturbance if they are unable to identify the underlying emotions from the range of feelings? Can we sort through our range of feelings in order to reach our true emotions? We know that identifying our emotions (not feelings) is critical, if positive change can begin. So how do we identify them?

Ellis developed his Rational Emotive Behavioural Therapy (REBT) in the 1950s, and created a formulation that makes the task of emotional recognition much easier. REBT identifies and focuses entirely on what Ellis dubbed the eight unhealthy negative emotions. The process seeks to replace unhealthy negative emotions with *healthy* negative emotions. This is not about taking people to a nirvana of denial and falsely positive happy places. It's reframing irrational beliefs, swapping demands for preferences, and formulating a healthier, more rational emotional reaction.

Here are the eight unhealthy negative emotions (UNEs) set beside the alternative healthy negative emotions (HNEs):

Unhealthy negative emotion	Healthy negative emotion
Anxiety	Concern
Depression	Sadness
Guilt	Remorse
Anger	Healthy anger
Shame	Disappointment
Hurt	Sorrow
Jealousy	Healthy jealousy
Envy	Healthy envy

We're familiar with the eight unhealthy negative emotions in the left column. They disrupt lives and create unhappy experiences and poor mental health. In the right-hand column are the alternative healthy negative emotions. These may be far less obvious. So, let's take a look at each one and the resultant typical *behaviours* associated with each one, to develop our understanding. Remember that our emotions govern the way we behave.

Unhealthy negative emotion	Healthy negative emotion
Anxiety Avoid the threat. Withdraw from the threat. Seek reassurance even though not reassurable. Seek safety. Avoidance behaviour.	*Concern* Confront the threat. Be realistic about the situation. Create a rational plan.
Depression Prolonged withdrawal from enjoyable activities and socialising.	*Sadness* Engaging with enjoyable activities and socialising after a short time.
Guilt Beg to be forgiven.	*Remorse* Ask (not beg) to be forgiven.
Anger Aggression. Lack of control. Unable to think clearly. Say things you later regret.	*Healthy anger* Assertion. Full control. Able to think clearly and communicate effectively.
Shame Withdrawing from others. Avoid eye contact with others.	*Disappointment* Keep in contact. Maintain eye contact.
Hurt Sulking. Not engaging. 'You made me sad.'	*Sorrow* Assertion (not aggression). Open communication.

Jealousy	Healthy jealousy
Suspicion.	Curiosity.
Questioning behaviours.	Brief questioning.
Checking.	No checking.
Restricting others.	Not controlling.
Need to control others.	
Envy	Healthy envy
Spoiling another's enjoyment of a desired possession.	Happy for them, but work to gain a similar possession.
'Why can't I have that?'	

Reframing Unhelpful Beliefs

Using my own ABC formulation would have enabled me to reframe my rigid beliefs so that my *anxiety* became *concern*. This would have allowed me to confront what I regarded as threats, as opposed to running from them. The issues were still there, but I would have seen them in a different way.

This isn't about denial. It's not about pretending that everything's okay. It is about changing the emotions that create the behavioural and physiological response, so that I could actively confront and (hopefully) solve the problem. I would have been more able to remember lines. The concern I felt, instead of being based on irrational fear, would have empowered me to think logically and realistically about the situation. To problem-solve rather than problem-avoid.

Let's look again at my situation:

A = Activating event/Adversity:
'I forget my lines and feel sick.'

B = Beliefs:
'I *must not* forget my lines. I *must not* let people down. I *must not* be sick.'
'It would be *awful* if the cast saw through my lack of experience.'
'I *cannot stand* the prospect of being seen as incompetent.'

C = Consequences:
Emotion: 'I feel anxiety.'
Behaviour: 'I become self-protective, quiet and withdrawn and want to run away.'
Physiology: 'I feel sick and experience sweating, a dry mouth, a pounding heart and memory lapses.'

Now, with more flexible beliefs, although the activating event remains the same, the consequence now changes along with my beliefs:

A = Activating event/Adversity:
'I will forget my lines and feel sick.'

B = Beliefs (once the ABC model has been applied):
'I would prefer not to let people down, but I accept that may happen.'
'It would be unfortunate if the cast saw my lack of experience – however, I can stand being seen as inexperienced, and will use this to learn as I work.'

C = Consequences:
Emotion: 'I feel concern.'
Behaviour: 'I am motivated to channel the nerves and learn from every experience. I will face up to situations. I will push on and learn at every opportunity.'
Physiology: 'I feel nervous but in control.'

We can see that with the beliefs disputed and reformulated, my behaviour aligns more to productive problem-solving and cooperative learning. That's my effective new response.

Now, the behaviour is not to run, but to face the fear, pushing on and embracing every opportunity to improve. I'd feel nervous, of course, and there's no harm in that. But the fear has abated, allowing me far greater control.

I may still have made the same decision ultimately: a rationally based decision that being a performer wasn't a life for me. But I would have at least made that decision in a more calm and measured way, without my personal struggle and the resultant physical ill-health.

By viewing difficult situations through a more rational, less rigid perspective, we change the negative emotions that we experience from unhealthy to healthy. This ability, which is the cornerstone of REBT, teaches many thousands of people to reframe emotions and therefore change the way they feel and behave. It's simply a life-changer.

You can start to use the ABC model yourself. Here's a blank example for you to copy and fill in, and you will also find it in the workbook.

The ABCDE Worksheet 📖 20

(A)	Activating event	
(B)	Beliefs about the event	
(C)	Consequences • Behavioural • Emotional • Physiological	
(D)	Disputing beliefs	
(E)	Effective new response	

Unhealthy vs Healthy Negative Emotions

Let's take a more in-depth look at the difference between an unhealthy negative emotion and a healthy negative emotion. The earlier table of typical behaviours gives some insight into the resultant behaviours, but a more detailed example may help. I've chosen *unhealthy* anger vs *healthy* anger.

Unhealthy anger invariably leads to aggression – physical, verbal or both. Nothing is ever successfully resolved when unhealthily angry. Any attempt will lead to shouting, hurling insults and possibly violence. Unhealthy anger eats away at us. We plot and scheme. We wish the other person ill. We disturb ourselves as we fume.

Consider this scenario: The audition is running late. You've been waiting for ages and are no nearer to being seen. Your levels of anger increase as the minutes tick by. Your inner voice takes over – 'How dare they treat me and other actors like this?!' – planning the perfect tirade to show the casting panel exactly what you think of them. You can stand it no more. You burst into the audition room and start to shout. Head pounding, thoughts jumbled, you're making a lot of noise, but not much sense.

Healthy anger, however, is about assertion. Whilst in a controlled state of healthy anger, we can be assertive rather than aggressive, leading to a discussion that's rational and calm. Clearly thought-through, salient points are now made succinctly and in a measured way. Healthy anger allows us to retain control, and therefore increases the likelihood of an earlier and more complete resolution of a dispute.

Healthy negative emotions allow us to reduce our disturbance and move forward in a rational, purposeful way. We still acknowledge that we're feeling negative emotions, but they don't trip us up. We keep control and manage situations on our terms.

The scenario now looks like this: The audition is running late. You've been waiting for ages and are no nearer to being seen. You go to see the coordinator to find out how long they expect you'll now have to wait. You calmly express your concern at the lack of information and suggest that more regular updates may be helpful. If the wait time is still long, you may ask if you could go to a nearby coffee shop to run lines. It's not ideal, but you're calm and respectful but assertive.

Here are other examples of behaviours that may stem from unhealthy or healthy negative emotion.

Unhealthy negative emotion	Healthy negative emotion
Depression 'I'm devastated that I didn't get the TV series, so I stay in bed all day, ignoring phone calls and emails.'	*Sadness* I'm unhappy not to have landed the TV series, so I take a day or two off and then start to engage with friends and family.'
Guilt 'My behaviour towards the director during rehearsals was unacceptable. If I plead, I hope she forgives me.'	*Remorse* 'My behaviour towards the director during rehearsals was unacceptable. I'll ask to meet with her to apologise, and hopefully build bridges.'

Anxiety 'It's the waiting at this audition that's dreadful. I've just thrown up, and I cannot remember a single line.'	*Concern* 'The waiting time at this audition is helping me to channel my nerves and run the lines so that I'm ready when the call comes.'
Shame 'I will never recover from getting the sack from the show. I'll avoid anywhere that I may bump into someone.'	*Disappointment* 'I'll get in touch with people so that I'm able to give them my side of the story that resulted in me losing the job.'
Hurt 'The way the director belittled me in front of the cast was so upsetting. I'm not going to speak to him unless I have to.'	*Sorrow* 'I'll find a moment to speak to the director about the way he spoke to me. I'd like him to know that I found it really unhelpful.'
Jealousy 'I was never happy about working with my partner. Now I'm sure that he's flirting with Titania. I think they're having a fling. I'm keeping a very close eye on them.'	*Healthy jealousy* 'There seems to be some chemistry between them, so I may have a calm word with him if it becomes too obvious.'
Envy 'I cannot believe that Stuart got the TV series. I'm much better than him. I'm utterly livid. I hope he screws up and ruins his reputation!'	*Healthy envy* 'It's great for Stuart, but it's also a sign for me to keep going, because it can happen to me too!'

Thinking Errors

Tied closely to our belief systems are the habitual thoughts that can trip us up and ultimately blight us. In CBT, these thoughts are called thinking errors or cognitive distortions.[3] We all experience them. It's part of the human condition. I was tripped up by several that I can now identify as errors, but at the time they were my 'truths'.

Cognitive bias exists because the brain can only use past experiences when we ask it to come up with a solution, a decision, or a simple choice. It serves us the information it thinks we require – but for two reasons, in doing so, it tends towards the negative. The first is because our brains operate on a system of threats and rewards, and will always lean towards the threat because that is our survival instinct. The second is because our brains give more weight to experiences that have an intense emotion attached to them, and sadly (in the West at least) we have more intense negative emotions than positive ones. For these reasons, thinking errors are essentially negative slants on the world that would not be borne out by evidence. And they often become stronger; in other words, our thinking becomes more irrational in times of crisis.

As an example of cognitive bias, this scenario may resonate: I've been sent by my agent to audition for a part in a play being directed by a person that I know of, but with whom I have never worked. My biased view is that there's little point in going, as this person *never* casts actors that haven't been to drama school. I formed this opinion because the only actors I know that have had any association with the director did all attend drama school. Therefore I may allow this empirically weak, cognitively biased opinion (my belief) to cloud my decision to attend.

But if I'm not at the audition, I will most certainly not get the job!

Here are examples of some very common thinking errors:

Magnification (*of the negative*)
'They'll all hate me.'
'I was absolutely dreadful.'

Minimisation (*of the positive*)
'Although Scene Three went well, the rest of the performance is bound to go wrong.'

Emotional reasoning
'This must be really bad as I'm feeling so emotional about it.'

Personalisation and blame
'The disastrous performance was all my fault (or all their fault).'

Mind-reading
'My director just ignored me. I can tell that they're angry with me.'

Labelling
'I'm a fool.'
'The stage management team are all idiots.'

'All or nothing' thinking
'I forgot my lines in Scene Two. That's it, it's over!'

Demanding-ness
'I must get this job.'
'You must learn your lines.'
'They should give us longer breaks.'

Fortune-telling
'I just know this audition will go badly.'

Overgeneralisation
'The project is a disaster.'
'These costumes are terrible.'

Low frustration tolerance
'I can't stand this backstage area.'
'I can't bear the producer.'

Phoneyism
'They're bound to see through me.'
'I'm not good enough to be at the National Theatre.'

Awfulising
'Oh my God, that rehearsal was awful!'

Exercise: Thinking Errors 📖 21

- How many of the above thinking errors do you recognise?

- Have a think about which ones tend to trip you up, both as a human being and as a performer.

- Note these down in your workbook, giving examples of when you have fallen prey to them.

Think about that last example of 'awfulising' a situation or event. We all have a tendency to see things as more awful than they are. Always ask yourself: 'How awful is it really, on a scale of 1 to 10?' A lost phone or unsatisfying rehearsal can seem like a 10, but set against a life-or-death situation they are probably a 2 or 3 – at most. Here's an exercise to explore an alternative response to awfulising.

Exercise: Awfulising

Awfulising can trigger unhealthy negative emotions such as anger, depression or anxiety. Awfulising-based rumination results in the replaying of dire scenarios that allow these emotions to deepen.

- A useful tool in tackling awfulising thoughts is to allocate a certain time in the day to *permit* yourself to think in this way. It could be fifteen minutes, or an hour. Whatever works best for you.

- Outside of this allotted time, you practise *not* thinking in this way. It takes time and perseverance, but as a therapeutic technique this method is used extensively and successfully.

My Thinking Errors

What was it that kept me in my state of anxiety? Here are the thinking errors and cognitive distortions that I experienced:

Magnification meant that I regarded my own inexperience as large, and other's condemnation of me as equally huge. This led to my feelings of *phoneyism*, otherwise known as 'imposter syndrome'. I was certain that everyone would see through me.

Mind-reading also came into it. As far as I know, I have no psychic powers, however I was convinced that I knew – just *knew* – what others were saying about me behind my back: that I was useless. That I shouldn't be there. That I was taking a job away from someone who deserved it more than me.

Fortune-telling was closely associated to my new-found, mind-reading 'powers', meaning that elaborate scenarios of being kicked out in disgrace were not only likely, but inevitable. All of this was happening in my head. I was the author of my disturbance. My self-sabotaging tendencies became a vicious circle. The more I thought in this way, the greater my fear and sadness became. My anxiety-provoking, self-destructive thinking became habitual, became my truth. It became me.

Awareness is the starting point of challenging these distortions. If you identified any of the thinking errors that apply to you, then you've begun your journey. By spotting the moment when you fall into the trap and by starting to question their validity, you embark on a journey to break the cycle. This new-found awareness allows reflection that in turn can lead to positive change.

Emotional Intelligence

You are aware that having greater control of your thoughts leads to healthier emotional responses – and this contributes to enhanced emotional intelligence. We looked at emotional intelligence in Chapter 1, to kick-start the process of becoming more self-aware, which is a key component to the process detailed through this book.

Emotional intelligence is also known as Emotional Quotient (EQ), and incorporates the main components of self-awareness, self-regulation, motivation, empathy and social skills.[4] As we said, it is a valuable accompaniment to the better-known Intelligence Quotient (IQ). In simple terms, IQ is the evaluation of a person's intelligence measured through a series of psychometric-based tests. Such tests seek to determine the level of problem-solving skills and memory ability of an individual, predicting, for example, skills suitability in a job role.

Emotional Quotient, describing the interpersonal and perception skills that we hold, is less formally measurable, and often misunderstood. However, EQ can be the personal performance, success, and happiness differentiator – and having a higher EQ benefits our general intelligence, competency and personal effectiveness. As psychologist Howard Gardner says, 'Your EQ is the level of your ability to understand other people, what motivates them and how to work cooperatively with them.'[5]

High emotional intelligence gives us a greater ability to effectively influence and engage others. It enables us to reduce our propensity to disturb ourselves, and with that comes greater contentment, motivation and focus. Clearly, these are really desirable personality attributes to develop and hone, both as performers and as people.

Many actors – with an innate understanding of their emotions and the ability to read those of others – naturally have skills associated with high emotional intelligence. The heightened level of empathy you harness to bring to life the characters you play enables you to engage people easily and effectively. You may also be very attuned to the subtle signs in others of, say, distress or impending anger.

If you need to, refer back to the outline of the five domains and the exercises you did in Chapter 1. At this stage, we would like you to start reflecting on your own abilities in each area. There is space in your workbook for you to make this an ongoing practice.

Self-awareness

A key attribute of emotional intelligence is emotional awareness: the ability to identify and name the emotion that you're experiencing. This is different to describing feelings. The awareness that enables you to recognise your own emotions, along with the ability to harness those emotions and apply them to enhance tasks like critical thinking and problem-solving, is very powerful.

Exercise: Identifying Your Emotions 📖 22

- Identify and name the emotion you are feeling right now.

- Then identify one other emotion you have felt in the last twenty-four hours, and assess whether this emotion was helpful or unhelpful at the time you experienced it and why.

Exercise: Understanding Your Self-critique 📖 23

- Alongside identifying emotions runs the ability to self-critique *constructively*, the very opposite of negative self-talk.

- On a scale of 1 to 10, how helpfully are you able to realistically appraise your performance? How well can you express and use this self-critique in a non-judgemental way?

- In Chapter 1, you listed your strengths and weaknesses. Refer back to this list and make any additions or changes. Now try to understand these strengths and weaknesses. For each of them, make notes that may include the following:
  1. How do they enhance your life?
  2. How do they cause you distress?
  3. Are the weaknesses really that, if you express them in a non-judgemental way?

4. Are the weaknesses areas of your life that you are able to accept, or are you prepared to commit time and effort to improve them?

Self-regulation

Self-regulation is your ability to manage your emotions and thereby respond in any situation.

Exercise: Understanding Your Self-regulation 📖 24

Spend a few minutes answering the following questions. You can answer 'yes' or 'no', numerically on a scale of 1 to 10, or you can give a fuller response. It is an exercise worth revisiting from time to time.

- Are you able to retain control in times of heated discussion?

- Can you use your emotions to positively influence the emotions of others?

- Are you aware of how much your moods and emotional responses influence your ideas and decisions?

- Are you good at managing any disruptive impulses?

- Are you able to take a step back and consider all aspects of a situation?

- Are you good at being reflective and buying time when this is helpful?

- How sincere do you consider yourself to be?

- How authentic do others perceive you to be?

- Would you describe yourself as trustworthy?

- Do you pride yourself on maintaining high standards of honesty and integrity?

- How easy is it for you to be able to admit when you are wrong, and apologise?

- Are you conscientious?

- Do you take responsibility for your own actions, or do you tend to blame outside factors?

- Are you adaptable? Can you handle change and retain flexible thinking?

- How innovative are you? How open to new ideas?

Motivation

In Chapter 1 we listed the three elements of motivation: Do you want the goal enough? Do you believe that you can do it? Do you believe that you deserve it?

Exercise: Understanding Your Motivation 📖 25

Spend a few minutes answering the following questions. You can answer 'yes' or 'no', numerically on a scale of 1 to 10, or you can give a fuller response. Come back to this exercise when you want to consider how your motivational drive is evolving and developing.

- Are you driven to achieve your goals despite facing obstacles and setbacks?

- Which of the three elements holds you back? (Do you want it enough? Do you believe that you can do it? Do you believe that you deserve it?)

- Do you strive constantly to improve, or to meet a standard of excellence?

- Do you keep to your commitments?

- Are you motivated to help others?

- Do you show initiative?

- Are you always ready to act on opportunities?

- Do you have exercises that you can employ if you feel your motivation waning?

Empathy

We hope that the exercise in Chapter 1 has helped you to establish a practice of empathy, and that you have developed the habit of walking in other people's shoes as often as possible.

Exercise: Understanding Your Levels of Empathy 📖 26

Spend a few minutes answering the following questions. You can answer 'yes' or 'no', numerically on a scale of 1 to 10, or you can give a fuller response. Return to this exercise to see how your levels of understanding and of showing empathy for other people are developing.

- Can you read other people's signals and react appropriately to them?

- Do you try to always see the world through the eyes of others?

- How far are you prepared simply to listen, and strive to understand?

- How much are you there for others when they need you?

- Are you able to empathise with those whose opinions are very different from yours, or who hold a very different worldview?

- Are you able to empathise with people with whom you have, or have had, a conflicted relationship?

- Do your empathy levels vary from day to day? If so, what do you think they depend on?

Social Skills

We hope that your social skills have improved through a reduction in the defensive responses that are the death knell to authentic communication.

Exercise: Understanding Your Social Skills 📖 27

Spend a few minutes answering the following questions. You can answer 'yes' or 'no', numerically on a scale of 1 to 10, or you can give a fuller response. You can always return to this exercise when you are feeling that your social skills are in need of further reflection or development.

- Do you have the skills to influence other people by using effective persuasion techniques?

- Are you able to inspire and guide people?

- Are you good at negotiating and resolving disagreements?

- Do you consciously build connections?

- Do you consciously nurture relationships?

- Do collaboration and cooperation come easily to you, allowing you to work with others towards a shared goal?

- Do your social skills vary from day to day, or depend on the group of people you are with? If so, think about why, and how you can work towards a greater level of consistency.

Conclusion

Many performers are naturally 'people people', and would tend to score highly on their levels of emotional intelligence – in terms of understanding both themselves and other people. But we are all more adept in certain areas than others. Think about the areas where *you* would like to improve.

The good news is that we have the ability to enhance our emotional intelligence. In fact, increasing EQ, as we said in Chapter 1, is a key theme of this book. Become aware of who you are and understand your strengths, but stay realistic about areas that would benefit from reframing and refocusing. This self-awareness will help you to identify which of the many techniques and exercises detailed in this book will be most appropriate to take you on your personal journey to enhanced emotional intelligence – and overall better emotional health.

7. *Brian on...*
Your Auditions

Performing is a form of public speaking. Based on their assessment of the evidence, the American National Social Anxiety Center has said, 'The fear of public speaking is worse than the fear of death.'[1] In survey after survey, generation after generation, speaking in public ranks as one of the top-three things people dread and will avoid doing at all costs. And yet still, a rare minority of individuals decide it is their calling to do this for a living. The additional psychological protection we have as performers is the character we have been given to play. This can be a powerful protection – many performers reference the shield that the character provides, which can help mitigate the anxiety response. There is, however, a critical stage before we gain the protective cloak of the character, and for many it is the most vulnerable and exposing part of our creative lives: being assessed.

For actors, even before we get the chance to perform in public, we have the significant hurdle of auditions to wrestle with. The white-heat intensity of auditions, with all the potential realities attached to the various outcomes, is like a heightened version of public speaking. The consequences of our ability to be successful, or not, in auditions can be catastrophic or transformative. How we approach and perform in auditions is deeply connected to how we view ourselves as communicating artists.

Your ability to demonstrate creativity, collaborative flexibility and captivating spontaneity in auditions can be developed by applying the following insights. This is the intention of this chapter: laying out a clear and concise route map for developing these three precious skills: creativity, flexibility and spontaneity. We will work to explore your current response patterns to audition anxiety. We want to determine the specific aspects you are happy or unhappy with. And we shall implement new habits to support behaviours that turn your aspirations into realities. Make notes for yourself – ones that both compel and inspire you to action – and be proactive in detailing what connects with you. Habits are formed through repetition until they become almost unconscious. Develop habits that support your ambitions.[2]

Let's explore how to tilt the audition odds in your favour by closely examining the tools needed to consistently function at, or near to, your best. To get regular work, stay healthy and to love what you are doing as a performer takes effort and commitment. At any one time, so the handed-down story goes, there is at least 95% unemployment in the acting profession. Auditions, either face to face or via self-tapes, are still the most prevalent way for work to be awarded. Your livelihood depends on you being able to handle the pressure in a way that does not stop you from giving of your best. Is it any wonder then, that this process has become a very serious stressor for even the most accomplished and busiest of actors? Indeed, some highly commercially successful actors believe that the work itself is deeply unhealthy in the emotional, physical and psychological demands that it puts on them as humans. 'Proceed with caution' should be the warning that all young performers are given.[3] *A strategy is needed.*

There is significant evidence that performers do indeed have a tough time of it in terms of mental and physical health.[4] Opinions vary as to the primary contributing factors, ranging from lifestyle, unsocial hours, higher inclination towards risk-taking and, of course, stress. The safe bet is to assume that they all play some part to a greater or lesser degree, depending on each individual. It is therefore vital that you develop effective techniques to cope with life as a performer, and the most frequent challenges you will meet. Auditions rank high on the scale of these significant challenges.

Often the anxiety experienced is in direct relation to the perception of how much the audition matters. Personally, I always felt more stressed when auditioning for TV or film, as I knew the possible material (i.e. financial) benefits would enable me to continue with the new-writing work that I loved doing. For whatever reason you think an audition is important, the debilitating sensations that overwhelming anxiety can bring are a huge part of the challenge you have to manage. Yet, *courage*, it can be done.

Your chances of audition success can be improved by following the techniques in this chapter, added to the cognitive training from the earlier chapters of this book. Actors who have mastered this process no longer experience stress or anxiety when they are being appraised or considered for work, only the 'excitement' pressure and 'performance buzz' we looked at in Chapter 2.

Exercise: Auditions Audit 📖 28

Let's make some notes on your current and recent audition experiences. Try your best to answer the following questions with honesty and speed.

- Do you have a professional, systemised way of creating readiness? (By 'readiness' I mean being in an optimum place physically, mentally and emotionally to do creative, collaborative and spontaneous work.)

- Are there things that regularly occur, interferences, that prevent you from being at your best?

- As you have read this book, have you already identified thoughts, actions or beliefs that are tripping you up in the way you approach auditions? (If so, keep these in mind as we move through the rest of this chapter.)

The answers to your questions are your snapshot of what your current approach to auditions really looks like. This honest appraisal and audit is the first step towards creating constructive behavioural change.

Now, I want to introduce you to a visualisation exercise. This will help you to be aware of the difference between what is currently happening to you in auditions, and what you would ideally like your experience to be. Think of it as preparing to prepare!

Guided Exercise: Preparing to Prepare ◀◙ 8

- Sit comfortably and close your eyes.

- Imagine you are in a waiting room or corridor before being auditioned for a very exciting production of your choice. It could be a film, a TV series, a radio drama or a stage play.

- Make it specific and desirable. Do not rush this imagining; let it emerge and be engaging to you. Perhaps use elements that you have actually experienced: locations, smells, faces, sounds. Build a meaningful scene and place yourself there.

- There are no lines to learn as you know you will be asked to improvise once you are in the audition room.

- Bring your attention to your breathing and then allow your thoughts to settle on the rhythm of your chest expanding and contracting, the flow of breath over your tongue and through your lips, and out of your mouth and nose.

- How long were you able to stay with the visualisation of yourself in that scenario? What happened to your own breathing whilst you engaged in the exercise? Stress, of course, takes us away from flexibility, making us rigid and closed. The exact opposite of what is required of collaborative, creative artists. The more frequently you do this exercise, the more you will be developing your ability to stay calm, balanced and ready to respond.

In order to make things accessible, easy to work on and enable real improvement, I created a framework that covered all aspects of the live audition process. (We will be looking at the process of self-taping towards the end of the chapter, although many of the techniques can be used for both situations.) The primary factors to understand, manage and develop are:

1. Your preparation rituals.
2. Your creative choices.
3. Your physiological response.
4. Your ability to be in the moment.

5. Your collaboration skills.
6. Your creative compatibility.
7. Your reflection time.

The only one of these not entirely within your gift to influence directly is compatibility, and even this can be made to lean in your direction. Each of these seven areas are to some degree interconnected. They all matter and can be enhanced through paying them close attention and taking focused action.

Your Preparation Rituals

Most of us have developed patterns of behaviour, ingrained over time, that become our way of coping or preparing for real-life challenges. Doing your daily physical and vocal exercises are a good example of this. With what we now know about neuroplasticity, it is important that our preparation rituals actually support us to function at our best.

The good news is that whatever is not working, we can change and replace with rituals that genuinely uplift us and give us the confidence to soar. These might certainly include the techniques we have learned through this book, and we'll suggest a few more here that may also help. Also, don't shy away from anything that has personal significance. By way of example, I have always incorporated singing songs that have special meaning to me before any challenging public-speaking event.[5] This has two positive impacts for me: firstly, it connects me with my sense of purpose and truth by way of song, and secondly, it prepares me for a higher level of communication which is how I look at the very best songs. 'These Arms of Mine' by Otis Redding never fails to get me in the right place for generous empathetic communication.[6] Find the songs that work for you and sing them at the right moment in your preparation routine. If you do not yet sing, two things: either start singing, or find words and phrases from poems, plays and speeches that really connect with you on an emotional level and align to your meaning and purpose as a creative. Say them out loud.

Here are a few suggested ingredients for your new ritual:

Two days before

See if there are any heavy demands that you are placing on yourself that can be swapped to preferences. Instead of saying 'I *must* get this job', swap it to 'I would prefer to get this job, but I accept that all I can do is my best.' Remember that we have to accept what is outside of our control. We might not approve of it, but we have to accept it. We cannot control the director's vision of the character (although I have known this to be swayed by an exceptional audition), or which side of the bed they got out of! However, we can make sure we do our best work once we are in the room.

The night before

Spend some time thinking about moments of real achievement and success that you have experienced in your life. Most of us are not great at acknowledging our accomplishments and using them positively to power our future success. Successful people learn from their mistakes and dwell on their achievements. Spend a few minutes revisiting your past successes in order to boost your confidence. This retelling of your personal achievement narrative is a great way to diminish unhelpful thinking.

Arriving at your audition

Begin a version of the Preparing to Prepare visualisation detailed earlier in this chapter, using the specifics of the physical environment as you find it. Focus on being present.

Just before going in

Do a quick mindfulness exercise[7] to bring down your heart rate and cortisol level, perhaps Image Breathing (from Chapter 1) and then a Power Pose (from Chapter 5).

Entering the space

Be aware of your body and make sure you focus on helpful and calming thoughts. Breathe deeply. Focus on being in the moment. Notice and acknowledge everything and everyone in the room, as much as you can. Listen with attention and keep your levels of interest, openness and curiosity as high as you can. Respond in the moment.

Your Creative Choices

Make creative choices that are authentic and true to you. It sounds easy, doesn't it? In essence, this is what the job of an actor consists of more than anything else. An actor that brings little to an audition and requires high maintenance to be creative is draining for everyone. It is far more exciting for a director to be confronted with a performer who is taking a clear direction with an idea, and demonstrating an aptitude for portraying truth, someone who is conveying passion.

Passion is what often disappears, without our awareness, when we are hindered by nerves. Have confidence with what you have prepared, what you know about the work and the character you are auditioning for. Of course, we all want to be as adaptable as possible to get the job, but somebody who agrees with everything, regardless of what is being said, is rarely hired. It's an easy trap to get caught in. Instead, be brave and trust your artistic instincts – take a clear direction with an idea and be prepared to accept collaborative suggestions to help develop it further as you audition. Having this sensitivity and openness is part of what makes the creative process so exciting and unique.

One cognitive bias we mentioned in Chapter 6 is *Personalisation*. This is where we see ourselves as the centre of the universe, and it's a bias that makes taking criticism, however constructively intentioned, incredibly hard. A lot of auditions are lost in a moment of defensive response, sometimes without the actor even being aware that it has happened. So, work hard to combat this. You need to develop your ability to take on board both healthy self-criticism and the constructive criticism of others. This can be a genuine boost for creative development.

Your Physiological Response

Become familiar with how you respond under audition pressure:

- What happens to your heart rate?

- Can you develop regulation of your heart rate through breathing techniques?

- What happens to your thoughts, and can you learn to regulate them?

- Think about the way your thoughts behave when you are under acute stress. Can you become aware enough to let unhelpful thoughts fall away?

- Remember that the extra energy surging through your body when you are feeling stressed can be a useful creative tool. Can you harness it constructively?

There is a real value in developing your understanding of the changes that happen to your whole body and mind when you are under stress. Being able to welcome stress – and make use of it – can mean looking forward to its appearance as opposed to dreading it. Many of our physiological reactions can be mitigated by the view we take of stressful events like auditions. Perception is everything.

Your Ability to Be in the Moment

There really is no substitute for being fully present, with your whole attention able to be brought to focus on the task in hand. This competency is at the heart of much creative collaboration. It is worth becoming attuned to.

Use the gateway of your senses[8] to bring your attention to right now: what you can hear, what you can smell, the visual beauty around you, your physical contact with the world, and the tastes you can experience. All of our senses can only be experienced in the present moment, and using them skilfully to bring conscious awareness to our lives is time and energy well spent. Presence is deeply connected to this ability to experience being here right now. It is worth cultivating.

Your Collaboration Skills

Another attribute that a director will be keen to see in an audition is your skill as a collaborator. They will want to know that you can take and share ideas and immerse yourself in a collective goal. And they will want to know that you are a good company member, a team player. Certainly confidence – as well as empathy, which we have looked at earlier in the book – plays a critical part.

Being really confident means that we invest more time and energy in listening to other people.[9] Insecurity or low self-image can be devastating for a collaborative process, and is often at the root of reactive and poorly thought-through behaviours. Most people like to think of themselves as flexible and accommodating, easy to get along with, and yet this can be hard to show at an audition. Stay in the moment, don't plan forward to give the audition panel what you *think* they want. Just respond authentically.

Sometimes the collaboration in auditions is poor because actors, frequently unconsciously, are too focused in on themselves. So, stay facing outwards. Keep your attention on the other people in the room and keep noticing things about each of them. You can even deploy your brilliant observational skills to snapshot their cadence of speech or movement patterns when they are expressing themselves. Use any technique that works for you to keep yourself from internalising your focus and energy. Keep watching and listening, and stay interested.

Your Creative Compatibility

This is where you have to be true to yourself and recognise that your process as an artist will sometimes be the thing that will preclude you from getting a job, and on other occasions it will rule you in and make the part yours. Look to develop an understanding of your preferred creative process, whilst also maintaining an openness to new ways of thinking and working.[10]

Do you like to be given a stimulus to use, or do you prefer to be given specifics about how to do something? Many actors respond well to ideas that they can use immediately, such as 'Walk into the room like the floor is electrified and you don't want to get a shock', as opposed to the director demonstrating physically how they want you to behave. What do you like best? Can you work with a range of approaches? Are you triggered by certain styles?

Think all this through for yourself. Think about when you have done your best work and what the given circumstances were for that collaborative process. Become very attuned to what has worked for you previously as a creative artist. Be specific about the details. Knowing what has worked for you in the past means you can start to hone your technique, whilst also allowing new methods to inform how you create. Being flexible in your approach is obviously a desirable skill to cultivate. We can sometimes surprise ourselves by trying something that we have never done before and seeing where it leads us.

A very good friend of mine, David Gaines, co-founder of a brilliantly innovative theatre company, the Moving Picture Mime Show, gave me a neutral, white, full mask as a gift. It was one of the tools that Jacques Lecoq (the renowned French auteur teacher of movement, character and acting) had pioneered in his work. David suggested that I use the mask to help to find the movement rhythms of any characters I was playing *before* looking for any other mannerisms, such as voice or accent. His simple idea was that the movement of a character could often suggest a voice that you would never consciously arrive at. This idea was always a great source of inspired creativity, and was something that I ended up using frequently and with great impact as a storyteller.

All of that being said, you still have to ensure that you are looking after your integrity and are able to preserve a sense of the value you bring to any project. There is rarely a positive outcome in pretending something is true just to get the gig. You have to be true to your authentic self, or the risk is you may end up in really miserable situations that compromise your integrity. Many actors have found out, to their disappointment, that the job they wanted above all else turned out to be something that did them harm psychologically or professionally. Conversely, the job they thought would simply be a rent-payer sometimes turns out to be the one that ignites their artistic flame and changes their life.

Your Reflection Time

After the audition, reflect on how it went.[11] Make note of any insights or thoughts that emerge from this valuable moment. Perhaps begin by asking yourself some of the following questions:

- What kind of directors do you like to work with, and why?

- What kind of direction do you like to receive and why?

- What kind of inputs trigger you in a negative way?

- What kind of inputs inspire you?

- How easy do you think you are to work with? And what are you basing this on?

- Is your creative process fixed and predetermined, or flexible and responsive?

- Is there anything about your current practice as a creative performer that is not serving you well in auditions?

Once you have spent time answering these questions with some real self-honesty, you will have deepened your understanding about yourself as a creative artist. The beauty is that your approach and competencies will evolve and develop. Committing to this set of questions can be a gateway for that professional growth. Much of what is suggested in this book can be defining; to be serious and committed to your chosen profession as a performer requires vocational focus.

If you do not cultivate the acquisition of the constructive habits we have discussed and shared in this book, it does not, necessarily, mean you won't be commercially successful. However, it may very well mean you are more susceptible to the industrial injuries that the performing arts can inflict on the unwary artist: drug and alcohol dependencies, toxic and failed relationships, and poor emotional and mental health.

The personal benefits of a sustained and constructive approach are well worth the effort. And this approach will increase your consistency, longevity and purpose as a communicating artist. Your perspective is needed and unique in the arts. Building your healthy habits is worth the investment of time and energy. By making this commitment, you will ensure you are able to contribute meaningfully over the long-term duration of your career.

Self-taping

The need for creative professionals to develop efficient and healthy skills around self-taping is only going to increase. As advances in technology have enabled affordable access to greater levels of near-broadcast-quality equipment, so the responsibility has landed on performers to be able to show their wares digitally. Let's separate these challenges into three parts: technical, psychological and emotional.

Technical Challenges

Is my equipment good enough?

Learn about what cameras, lighting and sound can do to help eliminate interference and allow the audience to engage with the truth of what you are looking to portray. The camera misses nothing and this clarity increases with the best equipment; however, remember the audience are engaged by the authenticity of lived experience being translated by you. What you choose to share trumps any fancy equipment. (As an example, take a look at the audition tape for the Steven Spielberg film *E. T. the Extra-Terrestrial* when they were looking to cast Elliott, the lead child character.)[12] Most phones now have cameras that are near broadcast-quality, and with an inexpensive tripod, some spot lighting and a decent pick-up microphone you will have more than you need. Focus on what you want to communicate.

Are the lighting and sound okay?

It does not have to be perfect; it just has to allow you to be seen and heard clearly and without any technical difficulties. Let's be honest, it is easy to get caught up in all sorts of avoidant behaviours because we want to put off the moment of truth. And that is all it really is: a moment that you are seeking to capture and send forward to be involved in a creative project. So, make sure you set up the equipment properly and get to the job in hand. Be in the moment, truthfully, and commit to act.

Am I set up in a space that is good for what I am doing?

This sounds straightforward, but be aware that some places and times of day are better than others. Think about the where and the when, and make choices that allow you to do your best, most focused work.

Have I allocated enough time to be relaxed in my performance?

Here is my rule of thumb: estimate how long you think it will take, all things considered, and then double your estimate and you will probably have just about enough time to do a decent job. That is my experience. You need to assess where your estimation/actual skills align and make the adjustments necessary. The most important aspect is to allocate enough time to execute it professionally, without allowing so much time that you end up ruminating and unpicking everything. Unproductive stress is your enemy here – and if you feel it is starting to take hold, then intervene and take a break or, if you have time, delay until you are able to regulate your feelings better.

Should I send the best technical take or the best performance take?

Most drama schools and production companies agree that performance is more important than technical aspects, though, of course, it is worth making sure that you have read the brief carefully and have a clear background. The cognitive bias (as discussed in Chapter 6) will apply to the director, and they may not even realise that they preferred the acting of the performer they could see more clearly. Always sending the best *performance* take should be your default position; they are casting a performer not a lighting or sound engineer.

Psychological Challenges

The two aspects of self-taping that we want to cover here are being too self-critical and doing far too many takes, and then not being able to choose the one to send.

Being too self-critical

Within the live audition process, it is not unusual for us to watch ourselves in this way. We should step away, know that we have done our best, and wait to hear. However, we may fall into the trap of playing the audition through in our mind, and finding that each time we hit replay, it seems worse. This, as you now know, is because of past noise. But the same can happen each time you watch your self-tape. Your inner critic may start to shout louder and louder. If so, skip forward to the Inner Critic, Inner Cheerleader Exercise detailed in Chapter 10. Train yourself to notice the positive. Each time you watch a take, ensure that you write down three positive aspects or qualities to the performance. Be consistent with this, even if it did not go well. *Especially* if it did not go well!

Making multiple takes, and choosing

If you find you are doing multiple takes, ask yourself this question: are you choosing to do it again because of the doing – it didn't feel right, you weren't really 'there' – or because of the watching? For most people, it is the anxiety about being judged by the future viewer that keeps them unhappy with what they have captured. We must have trust in our creative instincts. The process of increasing dissatisfaction feeds into our perfectionism, and can become incredibly addictive. It is also possible that you are allowing the way you look, or like to look, to colour your judgement of the performance. Try to be as objective as you can. We may think we are selecting the most powerful performance, but have actually chosen the one that makes us look slimmer/younger/more attractive. Most importantly, as soon as you become stressed with the process, step away.

Remember the Stress Curve from Chapter 2. If you move past that point of optimal performance and carry on, you are likely to think that the work you are doing is better than it is. Try to limit yourself to three takes. If you are currently doing way more than three, then set yourself a goal to reduce the number each time, until it becomes manageable. Or set a limit on the time that you are prepared to give, considering that you would normally have spent the time travelling to do a live audition. Create a success ritual around self-taping and stick to it.

Emotional Challenges

How are you feeling about the opportunity? What is going on for you more generally and how is this impacting the way you are feeling about your chosen career? Have you established some work/life rhythm, in order to support the tempo that allows you to work in healthy and sustainable ways? Have you prepared your mindset to be in the best place possible to share what you do as a communicating creative professional?

By answering some or all of the questions above, you will know where you need to place your attention to create the best possible readiness for you to be able to do great work. Then all that is left is for you to act.

Conclusion

The key to approaching auditions is to keep an eye on your long-term goal: your artistic career. Any audition is just a small step on your pathway. Keep swapping the demands you are placing on yourself to preferences; there's not many of us who don't pile the pressure on ourselves over auditions, unless we work very hard to keep it away.

The goal is to figure out for yourself what gets you into the optimum place – emotionally, physically and psychologically – to be ready to act.

Remember the director you meet wants you to be 'the one' because it solves their casting dilemma. Convince yourself that you are going along to see if you want the job. This will keep you open and attentive, and never desperate. And after the audition, be grateful for it, and then put it out of your mind. Don't allow the past noise to creep in and urge you to replay it because, as you know, it is more likely to serve up a negative slant on the audition than an accurate reflection of it. Instead, find at least one good thing that you did, congratulate yourself for it, and move on.

Everything discussed in this chapter can inform a unique and virtuous circle, helping you to actualise increasing success, however you perceive it. The seven steps begin with your preparation ritual, and end with reflecting on each individual step in the process. This then contributes to energise your next audition adventure. Create the habit.

8. *Brian on...*
Your Unemployment = Opportunity

David Bowie represented the optimism of possibility. I fell in fan love at about the age of ten when I watched, transfixed, on a black-and-white TV, as he lit up many lives performing 'The Jean Genie' on *Top of the Pops* in early 1973.[1] My young mind knew that if people like him existed in the world, then there was genuine hope that somebody like me could emerge from the chaos of growing up in a highly combustible, large Irish family in South London. My amazingly brilliant, eight-years-older sister was already a huge fan of Bowie and Marc Bolan. She had also somehow acquired a state-of-the-art sound system. I listened to everything that they created and the fascination with original artistic communication was planted.

There were many other contributing factors over the next ten years that propelled me along the pathway towards training as a theatre practitioner at Rose Bruford College in 1983.[2] At the time, amongst all the UK drama schools, it was the only full degree course available to aspiring performers. There were also some great people working as part of the teaching cohort. They had a vision for the future of the performing arts that meant they were pursuing an agenda of diversity and equality way before anyone else in this educational space. Without their vision, Gary Oldman, Stephen Graham, Ray Fearon, Bernardine Evaristo, and many other brilliantly talented, hardworking people would not have received their professional training there, in Sidcup.[3] I salute their courage back in the late 1970s and early '80s from the rear-view vantage point of today.

The vocational degree course was great in so many ways. That said, for the subject of this chapter, there was one glaring void: there was little or no preparation for the shocking and dramatic impact of unemployment that hit almost the entire cohort of my graduating class in 1986. Indeed, this reality is still true of almost every graduating class, everywhere, ever since. It took me thirteen months to find my first paid employment as an actor. During that arduous year I continued to live in my ground-floor flat right next to the college grounds. Every day during term time, I saw the current students going about their busy schedules and, of course, many of them were my friends. In the beginning, I was mentally healthy and looking to communicate and update everyone I saw about what was happening in my life. Almost imperceptibly, as time passed and without any career good fortune to relay to friends or family, I developed a horrible and all-consuming agoraphobia.[4] I seemed to lack the awareness of how to get out of this downward spiral; every aspect of my wellbeing started to decline.

With hindsight, it is clear to me that my training had prepared me very well for a world of work. But without acting work, I was literally clueless about how to cope as a creative artist in the world. I had gone from full-time, committed student, putting in eighty-plus-hour weeks, to suddenly having nowhere to be, week after week. There were other social, emotional and psychological factors in play, but the catalyst was my new daily circumstances, and having too much time to ruminate. I was not prepared for my new reality. I had to figure things out quickly and it took me a year to recover, to find my own personal Wellbeing Plan and to get well.

In this chapter, I will be sharing my framework for pursuing goals in a healthy and constructive way when there is no paid employment in your chosen profession. By going back to basics, I divided my waking life up into four fundamental areas that I called my 'planes of reality': the physical, the emotional, the intellectual and the spiritual. This approach became my route map for recovery, and I knew that I needed to stick to the plan if I wanted to have a real chance to make progress in the theatre industry. Please use whatever connects with you as a recipe list, to create your own plan and adjust as necessary, to suit the circumstances that you face. Develop and add to it as a practical and useful guide – and then pay it forward to those that come after you, in whatever way you can.

Your Wellbeing Plan 📖 29

The approach detailed below is logical and rewarding when adhered to. What happens, by the very nature of the profession, is that these healthy habits get kicked into touch when we are consumed with a work project. This is why they are so important to fold into your daily routines, so that you can reincorporate them seamlessly when time and unemployment arrives. And they can still be useful to reflect on and action when in work, if time and opportunity allow.

Physical

We all know that exercise makes us feel better and gives us a host of benefits. In case you need any more convincing, here is a list offered by the National Health Service in the UK, detailing the proven primary benefits that regular exercise offers:[5]

- Improves memory and brain function.

- Reduces feelings of anxiety and depression.

- Improves quality of sleep.

- Protects against many chronic diseases.

- Aids in weight management.

- Lowers blood pressure and improves heart health.

- Combats cancer-related fatigue.

- Improves joint pain and stiffness.

- Maintains muscle strength and balance.

- Increases lifespan.

When you are feeling dejected, however, and maybe even depressed, it can be the hardest time to find the motivation to begin exercising. This is where you must be firm with yourself and make a decision to act. Be true to what we are described as, and what we call ourselves: actors! We need to set aside time to be active every day.

Make decisions that commit you to action and doing[6]

Whatever it is: walking, running, swimming, yoga, dance classes or anything else that you enjoy and that requires movement. Commit to the activity and be open to making friends outside of the profession with whom you can develop activity-based plans. The key here is to choose things to do that you really enjoy. Remember, it is persistence and consistency that count. We all understand the temptation to buy the equipment for an activity, as if that means we are now actually undertaking it. Gym memberships are premised upon this sleight of hand. It takes around six weeks for the new routine, the new neural pathway to become your route of least resistance. Be smart and find activities that you can build a lifelong relationship with. Still to this day, cycling is my go-to reset activity, and it never fails to reward me with optimism, appetite, and a sense of amazement that it took us humans so long to invent the bicycle![7] And I am so grateful for its invention.

Eat food that is good for you

Closely related to exercise is the fuel that we consume to give us the energy to pursue our goals. Learning about nutrition is smart if you want to be ready for action as a performer. This is always true, but especially when you may have a lower income. Be creative and think up some cost-effective and nourishing meal ideas, and incorporate this effort into your daily routine. Just as important, try to avoid what's bad, particularly refined sugars and processed foods which impact negatively on mental health.[8] Use your new-found thinking skills to identify the toxic emotions: envy, anger, resentment, frustration, guilt, shame and overwhelming sadness to name just a few. These negative emotions can frequently drive the feelings that are leading to cravings and comfort eating. Try to recognise the emotional need instead – and address the cause. Remember the enteric nervous system, the 'second brain', which we looked at in Chapter 5: whatever is good for your gut is also good for your mind. And drink water – lots of it.

Sleep well every night

We have talked in earlier chapters about the importance of sleep. The conditioning influence of working late at night in the theatre can create dysfunctional habits around sleep and our ability to switch off. When you are not in the work you want, there is a real opportunity to look at your sleeping habits and make them healthier. Take the time to look at these rules of simple 'sleep hygiene', offered by the NHS, and build as many of them as you can into your daily routine:

- *Keep regular sleep hours:* Going to bed when you feel tired and getting up at roughly the same time helps teach your body to sleep better. Try to avoid napping where possible.

- *Create a restful environment:* Dark, quiet and cool environments generally make it easier to fall asleep and stay asleep.

- *Move more, sleep better:* Being active can help you sleep better. Remember to avoid vigorous activity near bedtime if it affects your sleep.

- *Confront sleeplessness:* If you are lying awake unable to sleep, do not force it. Get up and do something relaxing for a bit, and return to bed when you feel sleepier.

- *Write down your worries:* If you often lie awake worrying about tomorrow, set aside time before bed to make a list for the next day. This can help put your mind at rest.

- *Put down the pick-me-ups:* Caffeine and alcohol can stop you falling asleep and prevent deep sleep. Try to cut down on alcohol and avoid caffeine after midday.

The most important take-away from any sleep science lecture is that keeping to a regular sleep routine is essential for good emotional health. This is the hardest but most important goal to conquer when you are unemployed. Then, when you are approaching the start date for a new job, try to ease into the new routine, sliding the time you go to bed back by an hour every three or four days, so that by the time you begin the job you can hit the ground running.

Emotional

Being in-between performing work presents us with the opportunity to use the time to establish a solid wellbeing practice, both physically and emotionally. It gives you time to understand your patterns and triggers, and your areas of rigid thinking or limiting beliefs. All such self-knowledge gives you a clearer ability to understand the points of difference between you and any characters you will play in the future.

As well as the benefits we have outlined in each chapter, it can also provide a rich and deep world of creative ideas for you to draw upon as a performer. Time spent understanding your fundamental motivations will rarely be wasted. After all, before holding the mirror up to nature so that nature can see itself, the first place to start is with ourselves.[9]

Keep a journal and write things down every day

We have already talked about the importance of keeping notes on your process as you move through this book, but when you have 'free' time, jot down ideas as well. Of course, work hard to get your next job; however, don't spend all your time doing so – committing to self-development should be viewed as part of the career process.

This can literally be anything: a thought that occurs to you, snippets of an eavesdropped conversation that you grab while out observing the world, a memory of something significant from your past, a visualisation concerning something in the future. By doing this every day, you will be keeping in touch deeply with your internal emotional truth. You will also be collecting a body of ideas, thoughts, feelings and characters for your creative store. In *The Artist's Way*, Julia Cameron says, 'Be eclectic and annotate your feelings.'[10] This helped me to work out what needed my attention, and to remain connected with my thoughts and feelings about my place in the world, and how I wanted to contribute.

Go to see plays whenever you can

And build new pathways by watching the kind of plays that wouldn't normally be your choice. As hard as this can be, keep in contact with friends that are working and go to see their productions. Being supportive is a great way to stay connected and to boost your empathy levels. People will also remember and return the courtesy, and then it will be your turn to be supportive when they are in-between jobs. When you go, don't fall into the trap of critiquing what you see in a wholly negative way to prove (mostly to yourself) that you could have done a better job. Stay positive, supportive and constructive. In fact, avoid any stress-based, competitive conversations that are debilitating for everyone engaged in them. Think beyond the short term.

Intellectual

It is always important to stimulate your brain with ideas that help you to look at things in unique and different ways. Spending time with nature is also a great way to think about the incredible mystery of the diversity of our planet, and the multiple life forms that exist upon it.

Feed your brain with new ideas

Reading, looking at great art, and listening to the output of musicians is all part of this process. There is obviously an endless library of reading material about the performing arts, much of which has great value. Decide on three things about performing or about the industry that you want to learn, and then make a personal plan. Use this idea as a starting point for self-development. See where it leads you; the journey can be the reward. This may include taking workshops, attending lectures and seminars, or none of these. Discovering new ways of looking at things can have a positive impact on the ideas and knowledge you already have, deepening and enriching your perspective and practice.

Outside of performing, follow your passions. We all have things that have fascinated us since childhood, but we are yet to investigate.[11] Try to step outside the conditioning influences of your background and experience. Your brain will find creative ways to make use of the new inputs you feed it.

Make time to dream during the day

Of all the things in my Wellbeing Plan, this is the one that I have always found beneficial. By creating the space to literally do nothing, something magical sometimes takes place in your mind – it wanders creatively. On some occasions, it travels down alleyways that lead nowhere, and sometimes it comes up with flashes of inspiration that generate whole new directions and plans. We can, most of us, remember moments of fundamental insight that have come to us through 'daydreaming'. But keep a very strict eye on your brain. It is all too easy for the wandering to lead to the spiral of automatic negative thoughts, so make sure they don't take hold, as explained in Chapter 1.

A mind-wandering moment I remember well occurred in London's St James's Park in 1992. I had just finished reading *Blessings in Disguise* by Alec Guinness[12] and I started to daydream about charisma. Thoughts about people I had met and worked with who were clearly extraordinarily captivating started to occupy my mind. This daydreaming moment started to focus itself on a more philosophical, slow-forming question: 'Where does charisma come from and how can we engender it in people that don't seem to naturally have it?' Time passed and then my mind produced, almost from nowhere, a brilliantly clear memory: the face of a young baby smiling and entrancing a whole room of people with her energy. It was so simple and so clearly true: we are *all* born with innate charisma and the ability to be in the moment and connect powerfully with others. Today I know, with evidence from neuroscience,[13] that this is true, but in 1992 this insight fundamentally changed the way I looked at the world and the people in it.

Always try to note down these moments of creative insight, which should begin to happen more frequently because of your increased ability to be in the moment. It's hugely frustrating when gems are lost. Capture them; they are valuable. They are yours and you can gift them to others.

Spiritual

When I say 'spiritual', I am leaning on the part of the word that conveys aspects pertaining to meaning and purpose. I like this definition from the Earl E. Bakken Center for Spirituality & Healing at the University of Minnesota:

> Spirituality is a broad concept with room for many perspectives. In general, it includes a sense of connection to something bigger than us, and it typically involves a search for meaning in life. As such, it is a universal human experience – something that touches us all. Like your sense of purpose, your personal definition of spirituality may change throughout your life, adapting to your own experiences and relationships.[14]

Psychology Today, conversely, ascribes spirituality to cognitive bias, which we looked at in Chapter 6:

> As the brain processes sensory experiences, it naturally looks for patterns – and our conscious selves often seek meaning in those patterns. This can lead to the phenomenon known as cognitive dissonance which describes how, once one believes in something, one is strongly inclined to try to explain away anything that conflicts with it. Cognitive dissonance is not unique to religion or spirituality, but often occurs in the context of such beliefs.[15]

Take a moment to note down your beliefs and feelings about spirituality, and perhaps the impact it has on the choices and decisions you make.[16]

Live your purpose and higher meaning[17]

We have talked throughout the book about connecting with your 'meaning'. It is something we will revisit in the final chapter. Time between jobs can be well invested in exploring or deepening the meaning you have identified, as well as finding meaning in new things. Often, for example, it is time between jobs that we spend living a simpler life, and one that can lead us to find joy in the small things we might usually miss. Psychotherapist and author Sylvia Boorstein calls this 'awakening to the happiness of the uncomplicated moment'.[18]

A significant part of my recovery from mental ill-health in 1987 was involving myself in the Lewisham Vehicle Workshop. This was a vehicle-maintenance garage set up as a youth project funded by local councils to help young people with drug, alcohol and mental health challenges. I turned up without invitation one weekday morning and showed a willingness to learn about engines and the spray-painting of vehicles. I was welcomed and accepted. My intention was to reconnect with people from my own class background, and to function healthily in a supportive and non-judgemental environment. I also needed to commit to getting out of my flat and meeting new people outside of the closed world of the theatre industry. This experience helped me to discover part of my higher meaning.[19]

I have subsequently sought out multiple ways to contribute to assisting people in their learning and development. I have worked as a visiting lecturer/facilitator at many drama schools, universities and other educational institutions, and have always sought out opportunities to connect with people through shared learning. The more you do to understand your purpose, the more likely you will feel you are in control, and the catalyst of your own life changes.

Exercise empathy at every opportunity

As we have said previously, in this digital world it is very challenging not to be influenced by the narcissistic culture that the social media metaverse has super-charged. Understanding the lived experiences that other people are having is very difficult if you try to do it one step removed – in other words, digitally. Try to involve yourself in things that are happening in the real world. There's probably a host of things in your local area and some of them may be free: book clubs, film clubs, walks in nature, photography, choirs, whatever requires you to connect with other people, preferably outside of the industry. By embracing new activities and new people openly and with generous attention, you glimpse life through the eyes of those with a different perspective, and there is no greater way to develop empathy.

Conclusion

So, there you have the blueprint I have used diligently for the last four decades (gulp), since experiencing the mental health challenges of my early twenties. Staying healthy, in every sense of the word, is the goal. Through this state of readiness, you will be at your best when the opportunities you seek present themselves.

In addition to developing your own Wellbeing Plan, dedicate as much time as possible to the entire process detailed in this book. It's the perfect time to make strides because you are already at a crossroads, a turning point. So often a period of 'resting' leads to a slump in confidence and motivation. However, the opposite can happen. Take the opportunity to turn a corner – and don't look back.

9. *Brian on...*
Your Performances

In this chapter we will be examining the full spectrum of performance anxiety and assessing what the root causes of this debilitating emotional state really are. Rest assured, even accomplished performers have succumbed to some of the worst cases of 'the yips'. This term is most commonly used to describe a sudden and unexplained loss of ability to execute certain skills by athletes and sportspeople, but the same defence mechanism of the autonomic nervous system also impacts performers.

There are several incidents in which something happened in the mind of an individual and they made the decision never to return to live performing ever again. Three-time Academy Award-winner Daniel Day-Lewis, when playing Hamlet at the National Theatre in 1989, experienced an almost complete shutdown. In October 2012 he told the *Guardian*, 'I had to leave the stage because I was an empty vessel. I had nothing in me, nothing to say, nothing to give.'[1] To date, he has still not returned to any stage to give a live performance. An impactful experience indeed.

Let's try categorising the various anxieties to try to get to the bottom of what may be going on. Before we start it is worth remembering, as previously mentioned, public speaking frequently ranks as the number-one fear that people have in life. So, it is fair to say that many of us will already be hyper-sensitive about the pressure of performing in public. The other challenge to understanding any unwanted stress response is that we get no warning when an attack is going to happen, meaning we get no chance to practise our responses, as we can't fake a 'fight, flight or freeze' episode.[2] This is a significant part of the challenge in developing our abilities to cope.

Performance anxiety can be broadly divided into two main areas. The first is when we're doing what we normally do, and then for no obvious reason, the anxiety appears. The second is when we are thrown a curveball, and asked to do something new or unexpected. A common example of this is when understudies are called to go on with little or at short notice. Despite this being the nature of the job, it can result in enormous anxiety. We will look at this unexpected curveball first. Let's use an understudy situation to remind ourselves of the basic ABC model outlined in Chapter 3.

Exercise: The Resilient Understudy 📖 30

- Let's return to some of the same ideas as The Surprise Visit Exercise in Chapter 2, and imagine that you are the understudy on a big show in the West End or on Broadway, whichever is most engaging for you. Here's what happens:
It is the second performance and the person you understudy, the lead, is ill and unable to perform. You have just been informed with little time before curtain-up.
You have only had two rehearsals and have never rehearsed the end of the play.
The half-hour call has just passed and the company manager has told you that you are going on.

- You are going to consider two potential responses to the situation:
  The first is a non-resilient response – for example, 'It is the end of the world.'
  The second is a resilient response – for example, 'It may not be perfect, but I am positive.'

- Note down each response with your own ideas of how you could respond in the situation.

- At one extreme, the non-resilient understudy might actually refuse to perform, or even leave the building. At the other, the resilient understudy might see it as an incredible opportunity and count themselves lucky.

So, how might we use the ABC model to move from a non-resilient to a resilient response?

A = Activating event/Adversity:
'I have to go on!'

B = Beliefs:
'I can't do it! I'll be useless. I don't even know the lines. I'm not good enough to handle this challenge.'

C = Consequences:
'I leave the building, or hide somewhere. Or I stay physically present, pacing and getting more and more upset, and then begin a panic attack, unable to regulate my breathing.'

The aim is to reframe this to a new, more resilient way of thinking:

A = Activating event/Adversity:
'I have to go on!'

B = Beliefs:
'I can do this. The rest of the cast will support me. I am capable of meeting this challenge.'

C = Consequences:
'I will use the half-hour well, to check my lines and maybe ask a cast member or two to run the last scene. I will do my best. I will breathe and stay in the moment.'

Remember to accept what isn't within your control. You can't change the fact there has been little time to prepare and you have only had two rehearsals. However, by keeping calm it will ensure you are in the best place to turn in a good performance.

Rather than rigid beliefs ('I *must* be brilliant', 'The director *should* have given me more rehearsals', 'The audience *must* love me'), concentrate instead on the idea of *preference* ('I would *prefer* to have had more rehearsal time...') and the positive beliefs and consequence ('...but I accept I have been employed to do the job, and I will do the best I can.').

Fight, Flight or Freeze

Of course, what happened to the non-resilient understudy is that the 'fight, flight or freeze' response had kicked in. As we said in Chapter 2, this is instigated by the amygdala when we perceive threat or danger. In this case, it is the threat of failure or perhaps the loss of reputation, or even the destruction of a career.

We have added the 'freeze' response here, the rabbit caught in headlights, where any movement either towards or away from the danger seems absolutely impossible. Or the fear is so overwhelming that doing absolutely nothing seems the best way to ensure survival.

When the 'fight, flight or freeze' response kicks in, there are certain physiological signs, and these can vary substantially from person to person. Common symptoms are a tightening of the stomach or chest, dry mouth, sweaty palms, flushed cheeks and pulsing temples.

Exercise: The 'Fight, Flight or Freeze' Response
📖 31

* Take a moment to write down the physiological responses that apply to you when the 'fight, flight or freeze' response kicks in.

* The more closely you can identify them, the easier it becomes to feel the 'amygdala hijack' approaching, and with a little practice to be able to head it off.

* Make a note of when this last happened, and whether your response was fight, flight or freeze.

In reality, perhaps the most likely response you may experience in the context of performance anxiety is the freeze aspect – the 'shutting-down' that happens when the amygdala stops passing information to the prefrontal cortex. This is certainly true of the performance anxiety that can occur once you've entered the stage or are even in the middle of a performance.

Any of the mindfulness exercises detailed in this book can, of course, be employed to take you back to a space in which you can think clearly. A really useful one, because it is so fast-working, is STOP – a mnemonic that is easy to remember and can be done on the move:

S   Stop
T   Take a breath
O   Observe
P   Proceed

Observe whatever object you choose in close detail, notice everything about it – and hold this observation for six to ten seconds.

You need, however, to move to a state where you can be as confident as possible that the performance anxiety will not return. Regular practice of the techniques throughout this book will take you a long way to achieving this. You will gradually become more effective at managing your emotions and your anxiety in all situations.

For performance anxiety that hits during a rehearsal or performance period, it may also be worth you working to uncover what is driving the perception that you are in a threatening situation. You can start by asking yourself the following questions. Take care to answer as honestly as you can:

- Do I believe in the choices I have made with the character I am playing?

- Do I believe that my work as an artist has integrity?

- Have I prepared myself technically and psychologically to portray the human condition of this character?

- Have I found some meaning in the telling of this story?

- Do I believe that it is not about me and that I am here to serve the audience, or the playwright, or my colleagues?

- Have I gone through my normal 'preparation for success' ritual?

- Do I feel an unusually high level of scrutiny? If so, why?

- Am I in a good state of health – not suffering from illness, poor nutrition or exhaustion?

- What is the worst thing that can happen to me?

- If the worst thing actually happens, can I be okay with that?

Sometimes just an extra level of awareness can make us conscious of a threat that we had underestimated or even repressed. If you have identified such a threat, then start straight away to begin the work to change it. Again, give it time. Small steps are fine. Be patient with making progress. Consistency of practice is the key to success. We have to be vigilant in not letting our automatic negative thoughts run riot in any of the areas identified in response to the above questions.

The overall changes you are making will take a while to feed through to specific situations where there are long-established thinking patterns that support the damaging behaviours you have repeated in the past. Suffering anxiety during performance – or when thinking about performing – may have become your most-used pathway to which the brain will default when your defences are down. It will take time, as you know, for the new way of thinking to become robust.

One of the techniques we can use to speed up this process of change is visualisation. It works because, as we discussed in Chapter 4, our brain does not distinguish between real and imagined experience. Thanks to neuroscience we know that if we put a dancer in an MRI scanner and asked them to imagine they are dancing their part in *Swan Lake*, then not only would the same parts of their brain light up as if they were actually dancing, but the same muscle groups would also engage.[3] In the same way, an outcome-based visualisation can be used to help achieve any real-life goal; in this case, helping to conquer performance anxiety.

Guided Exercise: Goal-based Visualisation 🔊 9

Research shows that the clearer the picture you envisage during a visualisation, the more effective the process. It works best if you start with three key moments that you can fill with detail. You then go back and build an 'experience' or 'mental movie' by joining the three together.

We'll use the first performance of a new show that is causing you to feel anxiety.

- Begin by getting yourself comfortable in the same way as before – your hands on your knees or lap, your feet flat on the floor.

- Take a moment to feel the parts of your body connected with the chair or floor.

- Allow two good breaths and then close your eyes.

- We're going to spend a minute on each of three moments:
    1. As you step onstage for the first time.
    2. The middle of the performance, when you know it is going well.
    3. The curtain call, when you know you have done your best.

- For each of the three moments spend a minute creating all the details that you can.

- Now run through these three moments, keeping the level of detail – joining the three into a mental movie that you can replay over and over again.

Guided Exercise: Future-mapping 🔊 10

Another helpful visualisation is future-mapping, which is the process of visualising your future self. You will be considering who you will be when you complete your process of change and are no longer suffering from performance anxiety.

- Sit comfortably and close your eyes.

- Visualise that standing in front of you is a version of you that embodies the person that you could be – let's say in one year's time, when the anxiety is no longer a problem. They (you!) are glad to see you and they smile. Some people find it helpful to imagine a particular place as the backdrop or situation.

- Consider the following questions:
  What does this 'you' look like?
  How are they different from you now?
  How are they standing?
  How would you recognise their new-found strength?

- A whole new world has opened up to this version of 'you' because you are no longer held back by this debilitating obstacle.

- When you are ready, imagine that this 'you' turns so they have their back to you.

- Now step forward and merge into being them.

  You know now what they know.

  You know now how they conquered the anxiety.

  You know now what changes you will need to make for this to happen.

- When you are ready, step out and allow your future self to turn and to smile.

- You hear them thank you for making the changes that were necessary to allow them to emerge and to experience a whole range of new opportunities.

- When you are ready, open your eyes and know that you have already begun this process of change.

- Now repeat the exercise, this time focusing on the energy qualities of the person that you will become. How do they differ from the energy qualities you have now? Do you know why?

- After the exercise, open your eyes and remember the feeling, the posture and body shape, and the energy qualities that the future you possessed. Spend a minute walking around the space that you have, using the way that they held themselves physically and the energy qualities they most used.

Conclusion

There are two thinking errors, covered in Chapter 6, that are linked to performance anxiety. The first is perfectionism. Because we are driven by creative passion, we will often set unforgiving standards that we expect ourselves to achieve. But perfection can never be reached. Aim instead for excellence. There is almost nothing you can do that causes more stress than to set a goal that is unattainable.

The second is awfulising or catastrophising. If you feel the anxiety beginning then remember to ask yourself: 'How awful is the situation really on a scale of 1 to 10?' When scrutinised rationally, the number is likely to be lower than you might first think – and acknowledging this can help you to feel empowered and more able to reduce the anxiety to a manageable level.

Remember that change happens slowly and by consistently focusing on the outcomes we want and committing to the process. The direction of travel is what matters. Over time, new ways of thinking, feeling and doing will take root. Trust your intentionality.[4]

10. *Beth on...*
Your Enjoyment

And so we enter the final part of the book. This chapter is about acknowledging what has already changed, and about setting the goals that will help you to keep moving forward.

I'm going to repeat the Emotional Audit that we did in the very first chapter. After you have done the audit, take a little while to dig in deep and look at anything that has changed, and think about the reasons why. Changes to the way we think and feel happen gradually, so it is often only through a process of audit and reflection that we realise how much we have actually changed. I certainly didn't do this nearly enough at the very beginning of my journey developing my emotional health. It was only when several people commented on how calm I had become, that I really started to mark my progress so that I knew exactly where I was.

Exercise: Emotional Audit Follow-up 📖 32

- Draw four columns like the table below or find the template in your workbook:

Emotion	Level of Intensity	Experience	Possible Cause

- Now spend ten to fifteen minutes completing the table by listing every emotion you know you have felt (or think you might have felt) in the last week; the level of intensity with which you experienced it; whether it was a positive or negative sensation/ experience; and what you think might have caused it. Finish by putting a star by any of them that you are worried about.

- Compare this with the audit you did in Chapter 1. Consider whether the way you see yourself, other people and the world has changed. Perhaps you have already begun the process of moving from mind-wandering to mind-wondering?

The Four-Stage Process

The time when you have been reading this book has been a period of *awareness*, which is the first of the four stages required to permanently change the way we respond to the world. Now we need to consider all four stages as a step plan:

Awareness

The first stage is simply awareness. You will already have attained a deeper level of consciousness about your thinking, and the way it changes how you feel. And you know that often deeper inspection is required because although what you are thinking feels absolutely right, it may not be logical, helpful or even true.

Labelling

The second stage is labelling. If you haven't already, try to identify your specific 'types' of negative thinking, whether this be negative self-talk, past or future noise, or one of the thinking errors detailed in Chapter 6. If you know, for example, that you fall prey to low frustration tolerance then you are much more likely to 'see' it as it comes onto your cognitive horizon. You may even be able to evade it entirely before it takes hold.

Monitoring

The third stage is monitoring. Make a note of when each type of negative thinking comes. Note the thoughts that lead to the negative 'invasion', and your emotional state in the preceding minutes. It is likely that you will very quickly start to see patterns and triggers.

Reframing

Once you are at this fourth stage, all of your negative thinking can be reframed using the ABC model. I recommend that you do a mindfulness exercise first to clear any emotional entanglements.

We find this four-stage process to be incredibly effective, though for a small minority the awareness itself is enough to effect really significant change. The key is to catch the negative thought the second that it happens and to do this consistently. A very simple exercise to help you to do this is Catch and Throw.

Exercise: Catch and Throw

- As the automatic negative thought enters your mind, say it out loud, and catch it in your hand.

- Turn your hand while taking a breath.

- 'Throw' the thought away from you whilst saying the positive or reframed version.

For example, the negative thought might be 'Jim ignored me by the stage door. I don't think he likes me.' The reframed version to vocalise as you throw away the negative thought might be 'Jim looked like he was struggling by the stage door this morning. I wonder if I can do anything to help.'

The reason you say the thought out loud as you catch it is because if you have said the same thing, or almost the same thing, ten times in a week you will definitely notice the pattern!

Moving Forwards

You should set some goals that will help you in keeping your commitment to unlocking your emotional wealth. Back in Chapter 1 you identified your meaning. Aligning your goals, your beliefs and your meaning is key to stopping the self-sabotage that most of us fall prey to.

Your Goals, Beliefs and Meaning

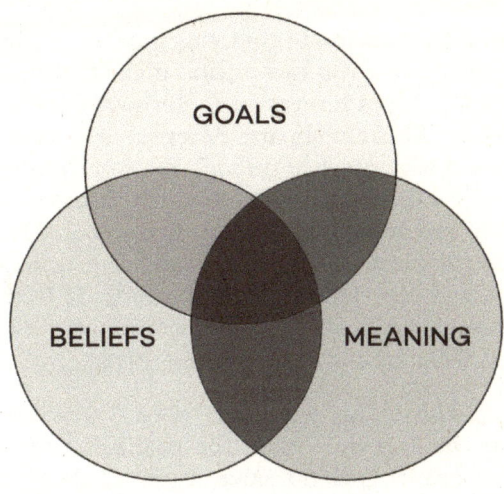

Many people have beliefs and meaning that have nothing to do with their daily life, or even hold beliefs that run totally counter to what they do in their day-to-day existence. For example, they may believe in the absolute equality of every individual, but this is not informing any part of their lives. No activities they undertake have any connection with this belief. Or worse, they may be working for an organisation that perpetuates a rigid and damaging hierarchical structure.

Start by revisiting the meaning you identified in Chapter 1. If you find it has changed, acknowledge that now. Then think about goals that you have that tie in with your meaning. For example, if you believe that the overarching inequalities within the performance industry need to be addressed, think about what *you* can do that would further this cause, work towards *your* meaning. Goals will always change as life moves forward and you take on new priorities. Consciously changing your goals is fine; neglecting or abandoning them is not.

My meaning comes from promoting inclusivity and better mental health, so I run two organisations that tie in with this meaning: Mind Fitness for Performers and Prospero, an inclusive theatre company. My goal is to spread and develop inclusive practice through the work of these two organisations. But with that identified meaning around inclusivity and mental health I could also be a fundraiser for a mental health charity, or a teacher in a school for students with special educational needs. It is thinking about how your goals best fit in with your skills (or potential skills) and your motivating drive.

Napoleon Hill in his wonderful book *Think and Grow Rich* uses the analogy of the main goal being like a boat. For every smaller goal, objective or proposed task you ask yourself 'Is it helping the boat to go faster?' For example, we have been asked twice to take part in high-profile projects indirectly linked to our process. They have been tantalisingly attractive, but we have turned them down because we did not believe they would 'make the boat go faster'; they would not further our main goal of helping as many people as possible to better mental and emotional health.

Exercise: Goal-based Visualisation II

Once you have identified your main goal which is tied as firmly as possible to your meaning then do a Goal-based Visualisation, as we did in Chapter 9.

- Start by identifying three key 'moments' at the beginning, middle and end of the journey, and then create a mental movie that links them through.

- The more you play this movie, the more you are preparing your brain for the successful accomplishment of the goal.

Linked to your meaning and motivation, try to build doing something meaningful into your new life plan.

My inclusive theatre company Prospero has many volunteers, two-thirds of whom have a disability. This came about because our first learning-disabled volunteer Drew said, 'All my life I have been given to, and this is the first time I have had the opportunity to give something back.' I had, until that point, underestimated the profound importance of this.

Doing something on a regular basis that helps others can help to keep you motivated towards achieving your other goals, as well as giving an enormous boost to your self-image. You will know that you are living your values.

Your Self-image

To achieve the goals that you have set out for yourself, a positive and robust self-image is key. Self-image literally determines the way that we see not only ourselves but the outside world, and the way we respond to it. We have to believe in ourselves, to believe that we can achieve and commit.

Remember the definition that we used for stress back in Chapter 2. Stress occurs when our perceived pressure exceeds our perceived ability to cope. To a very large extent if we believe that we are able to do something then we will. It's like the Confucius quote: 'The man who says he can, and the man who says he cannot, are both correct.'

We're going to start by doing a very simple exercise in which we turn our inner critic into an inner cheerleader.

Exercise: Inner Critic, Inner Cheerleader 📖 33

- On a sheet of paper or in your workbook, draw two large circles or ovals. Above the circle on the left write 'Inner Critic', and above the other write 'Inner Cheerleader'.

- In the Inner Critic circle, write any of the negative self-talk statements that you have identified as you have moved through the book – the harsh statements that we say about ourselves, and often deeply believe. These can, as you will know, vary from the seemingly trivial and harmless ('I'm useless with tech') to the deeply damaging ('I am a bad friend' or 'I hate myself'). Even the trivial self-talk erodes our self-image, and therefore our abilities over time.

- Now in the Inner Cheerleader circle you are going to take each self-talk statement and turn it on its head – and make it into an 'I can' statement, a positive affirmation. For example, you might turn 'I cannot cope in auditions' into 'I am now coping well with auditions.' If it's too big a jump (for example, to move from 'I hate myself' to 'I love myself') then make a statement that is an easier leap, such as 'I did well with sorting my life admin on Tuesday' or 'I was kind to my partner today.' Then, over time, work to go the rest of the way. It doesn't matter how many jumps you need to get you to the target cheerleading statement.

All too often we listen to our negative self-talk and allow it to determine our self-image. Of course, to have negative self-talk is part of the human condition, but we don't have to listen to it.

Your negative self-image may come from the feeling that you shouldn't boast, shouldn't stand out. People outside the performing arts would perhaps be surprised that this is true of performers. But it is certainly true that many play down the most exquisite of performances they have delivered, and the most enviable of talents. For good emotional health, we must accept, really accept, that holding a low opinion of ourselves isn't a virtue but a *vice*.

Your Self-value

When working on self-image we suggest that you think in terms of self-value rather than the more common concept of self-esteem. This is because to esteem is to weigh up in a way that is necessarily both relative and conditional; in other words, self-esteem is relative to the value of other people (which we see the results of every day on social media) and conditional upon, say, the job or agent you have, the money you earn, or the reviews for your last show.

If our self-value depends on external events or people, then we are vulnerable. Many people when they are made redundant – or in the performing arts when a long contract ends – are crushed, because they have bound up their self-value, even their identity, with their role.

It's easy to see how this relates in so many ways to performers. If we are not careful, our self-image will be constructed around our current or most recent job (or even our last audition), and this is a very unsteady foundation for something so important. It is easy to fall into the situation described in author Deepak Chopra's wise words: 'When you're happy for a particular reason you are still in misery, because that reason can be taken from you tomorrow.'[1]

Instead, try to build a strong sense of self-value that is based on unconditional self-acceptance. Recognise the many positive facets of your personality, and the value you give to those close to you and the wider world. Start by making a list of all the positive beliefs you have about yourself, and keep adding to it each day. We all have hundreds of positive beliefs about ourselves and others, but for a large part they lie buried and untapped. Bring them to the front of your life, where they can powerfully drive a positive self-image and your commitment to change.

Your Achievements

It is of vital importance that you acknowledge and celebrate your successes. I recommend that you keep a simple corkboard or whiteboard somewhere in your house on which you can pin up or write down your achievements.

It's a wonderful place to stand and reflect when you need a little extra motivation, and I find it a good way of monitoring my emotions. If I haven't pinned up anything for a few days, I probably need to think about why.

Your Emotional Health Plan

It's time to develop an emotional health plan for yourself, which draws together the techniques and exercises you will continue to use moving forwards. It needs to be easy to maintain, and personalised for you, so feel free to adapt it and to incorporate the techniques that you think are most appropriate to where you are and where you want to be. It's very likely that during the time that you've been reading this book there will be exercises that have resonated most with you, and have worked best for you personally. Those are the ones to include!

I would, however, recommend that you incorporate some mindfulness practice into your plan. Not only does it bring down the level of cortisol and quietens the noise in your brain, but it's essential to creating the space in which you can make the big changes that you want to see happen. It helps you to stop defending your old thoughts and actions long enough to embrace the new.

Here's what your emotional health plan might look like. Your workbook contains a template plan for you to complete. 📖 34

Daily (ten minutes a day)

- A mindfulness exercise each morning and each evening. Choose any of the exercises detailed in the book.

- A gratitude exercise each morning and each evening. In the morning simply make a list of three things that you're grateful for and in the evening make a list of three things that you're grateful for that have happened that day.

Weekly (one forty-minute session)

- Select a negative unhelpful belief and reframe it using the disputing technique outlined in Chapters 3 and 6.

- Pick a cognitive bias listed in Chapter 6 that you fall prey to and do the following three-step exercise:

1. Create a sentence stating the belief (e.g. 'I cannot bear waiting in queues').
2. Create a sentence stating the opposite (e.g. 'I love waiting in queues').
3. Create a sentence finding the middle ground (e.g. 'I am fine waiting in a short queue once a week').

The Rest of the Week

- You are with your brain 24/7. During the rest of your week you should simply be aware of what you are thinking, and try and follow the four-stage process of: awareness – labelling – monitoring – reframing.

- Recognise demands and swap them down to preferences.

- Recognise the automatic negative thoughts as soon as they come, and do either a mindfulness exercise or Catch and Throw.

- Recognise moments of awfulising and ask yourself, 'How awful is it really on a scale of 1 to 10?' Train yourself not to sweat the small stuff! It can be done.

Your Enjoyment

For all the reasons we have outlined throughout this book, as a performer you are in a very strong place to make changes that will positively impact your mental and emotional health. It is likely that you already have heaps of resilience, creativity and compassion. It is just about making sure that, as well as being the tools of your trade, they are tools that will help you to build a calmer and happier life for yourself.

Of course, persistence is key. You will always have doubts, but hold faith with the plan and get yourself back on track as quickly as you can. No one ever goes from point A to point B in a straight line. Even the most successful people zigzag their way from one to the other. It is getting yourself back to the line as quickly as possible that counts. Those who are successful are adept at this art of 'course-correcting'.

Know your destination and enjoy the journey. Most people who begin any process of self-development are hoping that it will help them feel better for more of the time. And it absolutely will. As we said in the opening chapter, misery is optional, happiness is optional.

Let's end with gratitude. It is simply the process of noticing what you do have, rather than noticing what you don't have. Your brain cannot think a negative thought and feel grateful at the same time. So, if there are times when none of the techniques seem to be working, just focus your mind on something or someone for whom you feel profoundly and sincerely grateful. It's a powerful tool to take you towards a 'glass half-full' mindset. If you follow the techniques set out in the book, this, perhaps, is the reward. And it isn't about wishing or pretending the glass was half-full, it is about looking for the evidence and seeing that it really *is*. Enjoy the world from a perspective of emotional wealth.

You chose this profession because it is extraordinary – and *you* are extraordinary. So, enjoy it. Take the techniques that you have discovered and embed them into your life. Aim high. Now is the time to stop the self-sabotage and to unlock your true potential. And, if you can, be the guiding light for others. The more performers that attain a state of emotional wealth, the higher the creative bar can be raised. It's *all* to play for.

References

Introduction

1. Sussex MSK Partnership (2024), *Health & Wellbeing (Emotional Wellbeing) – Sussex MSK Partnership* [online], available at: sussexmskpartnershipcentral.co.uk/health-wellbeing-emotional-wellbeing/#:~:text=What%20is%20Emotional%20Wellbeing?

2. Richter, D. (1949), *Homepage – UK and England* [online], www.mentalhealth.org.uk, available at: mentalhealthfoundation.org.uk

3. Barker, A. and Cooley, B. (2024), *Mind Fitness – Mental Health, Wellbeing & Personal Effectiveness Courses* [online], Mind Fitness, available at: mindfitness.training

4. Wood, B. (2015), *Mind Fitness for Performers* [online], Prosperotheatre.net, available at: prosperotheatre.net

5. Passingham, R.E. and Wise, S.P. (2012), *The Neurobiology of the Prefrontal Cortex*, Oxford: Oxford University Press

6. Harvard Business Review, McKee, A., Grant, H., Achor, S. and Elizabeth Grace Saunders (2022), *Energy + Motivation (HBR Emotional Intelligence Series)*, Boston, MA: Harvard Business Review Press

2: Your Resilience

1. Dr Alia Crum at Stanford University

3: Your Brain

1. Helmstetter, S. (2014), *The Power of Neuroplasticity*, CreateSpace Independent Publishing Platform

2. Ellis, A. and MacLaren, C. (2005), *Rational Emotive Behavior Therapy: A Therapist's Guide*, Atascadero, CA: Impact Publishers

3. Neenan, M. and Dryden, W. (2013), *Life Coaching*, Abingdon: Routledge

4. Dryden, W. (2010), *Dealing with Clients' Emotional Problems in Life Coaching*, Abingdon: Routledge

5. Helmstetter, *The Power of Neuroplasticity*

4: Your Imagination

1. Benzon, H.T., Prithvi Raj, P., ScienceDirect [online] and Al, E. (2008), *Raj's Practical Management of Pain*, Philadelphia, PA: Mosby-Elsevier

2. Cambridge Dictionary (2024), 'sickie' [online], CambridgeWords, available at: dictionary.cambridge.org/dictionary/english/sickie

3. Csikszentmihalyi, M. (1997), *Creativity: Flow and the Psychology of Discovery and Invention*, New York, NY: HarperCollins Publishers

4. Kabat-Zinn, J. (2013), *Full Catastrophe Living, Revised Edition: How to cope with stress, pain and illness using mindfulness meditation*, London: Piatkus

5. Moore, S. (1998), *Stanislavski Revealed: The Actor's Guide to Spontaneity on Stage*, New York, NY: Applause Theatre Books

5: Your Body

1. van der Kolk, B. (2014), *The Body Keeps the Score: Brain, Mind, and Body in the Healing of Trauma*, London: Penguin Books

2. Gershon, M.D. (1999), *The Second Brain: A Groundbreaking New Understanding of Nervous Disorders of the Stomach and Intestine*, New York, NY: HarperCollins World

3. Cuddy, A. (2012), *Your Body Language May Shape Who You Are* [online], www.ted.com, available at: ted.com/talks/amy_cuddy_your_body_language_may_shape_who_you_are?subtitle=en, and Cuddy, A. (2020), *Presence*, London: Orion

6: Your Emotions

1. Ellis, A. (2010), *Rational Emotive Behavior Therapy*, Amherst, NY: Prometheus Books

2. *Ibid.*

3. Beck, A.T. (1976), *Cognitive Therapy and the Emotional Disorders*. New York, NY: Penguin Books

4. Harvard Business Review and Goleman, D. (2015), *HBR's 10 Must Reads on Emotional Intelligence (with featured article 'What Makes a Leader?' by Daniel Goleman)(HBR's 10 Must Reads)*, Boston, MA: Harvard Business Review Press

5. Gardner, H. (2006), *The Development and Education of the Mind*, Abingdon: Routledge

7: Your Auditions

1. nationalsocialanxietycenter (2015), *National Social Anxiety Center* [online], available at: nationalsocialanxietycenter.com

2. Franklin, B. and Unique Journal (2017), *By Failing to Prepare You Are Preparing to Fail*, CreateSpace Independent Publishing Platform

3. Maher, K. (2020), 'Julie Walters: "I don't want to work again… unless there's a *Mamma Mia 3*"' [online], *The Times*, available at: thetimes.com/culture/film/article/julie-walters-i-dont-want-to-work-again-unless-theres-a-mamma-mia-3-fdn0dxsn3

4. Google.com (2020), *science direct volume 253 inequalities in life* [online], available at: google.com/search?q=science+direct+volume+253+inequalities+in+life&rlz=1C1CHBF_en-GBGB908GB908&oq=science+direct+

volume+253+inequalities+in+life&gs_lcrp=EgZjaHJvb
WUyBggAEEUYOTIGCAEQRRg80gEKMTQwNDlq
MGoxNagCCLACAQ&sourceid=chrome&ie=UTF-8

5. Meyer, T. H. (2016), *A Life of Creative Purpose*, CreateSpace Independent Publishing Platform

6. Otis Redding, 'These Arms of Mine' (Official Music Video) [online], available at: youtu.be/GVbTE4wCbpw

7. *Mindfulness (HBR Emotional Intelligence Series)* (2017), Boston, MA: Harvard Business Review Press

8. Heidegger, M., Emad, P. and Kalary, T. (2016), *Mindfulness*, London: Bloomsbury Academic

9. Messner, W. (2013), *Intercultural Communication Competence: A Toolkit for Acquiring Effective and Appropriate Intercultural Communication and Collaboration Skills*, Bangalore: Global Research

10. Robinson, S.K. (1151), *Do Schools Kill Creativity?* [online], www.ted.com, available at: ted.com/talks/sir_ken_robinson_do_schools_kill_creativity?subtitle=en

11. Guinness, A. (1985), *Blessings in Disguise*, London: Hamish Hamilton

12. 'Henry Thomas audition for E.T. "Ok kid, you got the job".' [online], available at: youtu.be/tA5giyG8E7g

8: Your Unemployment = Opportunity

1. Songfacts (2020), '"The Jean Genie" by David Bowie – Songfacts' [online], Songfacts.com, available at: songfacts.com/facts/david-bowie/the-jean-genie

2. Rose Bruford (2024), 'Get in touch – Rose Bruford' [online], available at: bruford.ac.uk/about/contact-us

3. Rose Bruford (2024), 'Alumni – Rose Bruford' [online], available at: bruford.ac.uk/careers-industry/famous-alumni

4. Hurst, R. (1986), *Agoraphobia*, London: Faber and Faber

5. NHS Choices (2020), 'Benefits of exercise' [online], available at: nhs.uk/live-well/exercise/exercise-health-benefits

6. Harris. R. and Hayes, S. (2008), *The Happiness Trap,* London: Robinson

7. Wikipedia contributors (2019), 'History of the bicycle' [online], Wikipedia, available at: en.wikipedia.org/wiki/History_of_the_bicycle

8. Cediel, G., Rauber, F., Mendonca, A., Meireles, A., Alvim Leite, M. and Gombi-Vaca, M. (2023), *Ultra-Processed Foods and Human and Planetary Health,* Frontiers Media, SA

9. Shakespeare, W., *Hamlet,* Act III, Scene II

10. Cameron, J. (2014), *The Artist's Way,* London: Souvenir Press

11. Hallowell, E. M. (2024), *The Childhood Roots of Adult Happiness,* Penguin Random House [online], PenguinRandomhouse.com, available at: penguinrandomhouse.com/books/73947/the-childhood-roots-of-adult-happiness-by-edward-m-hallowell-md

12. Guinness, *Blessings in Disguise*

13. Burnham, C. and Mars+Design (2011), *The Charisma Edge,* CreateSpace Independent Publishing Platform

14. Millman, D. (2016), *Four Purposes of Life: Finding Meaning and Direction in a Changing World,* Novato, CA: H J Kramer

15. Festinger, L. (1957), *A Theory of Cognitive Dissonance.* Stanford, California: Stanford University Press

16. *Psychology Today* (2019), 'Psychology Today Canada: Health, Help, Happiness + Find a Therapist CA' [online], Psychology Today, available at: psychologytoday.com

17. Gillam, A. J. and SpringerLink (online service) (2018), *Creativity, Wellbeing and Mental Health Practice,* Cham: Springer International Publishing

18. Boorstein, S. and Fisher, N. (2007), *Solid Ground: Buddhist Wisdom for Difficult Times,* Berkeley, CA: Parallax Press

19. Delagran, L. (2019), *What Is Spirituality? Taking Charge of Your Health & Wellbeing* [online], Taking Charge of Your Health & Wellbeing, available at: takingcharge.csh.umn.edu/what-spirituality

9: Your Performances

1. Peter Stanford (2008), 'The Enigma of Day-Lewis' [online], *Guardian*, available at: theguardian.com/film/2008/jan/13/awardsandprizes.danieldaylewis

2. Everly, G. S. and Lating, J. M. (2019), *A Clinical Guide to the Treatment of the Human Stress Response*, New York, NY: Springer

3. Sheikh, A. A. and Korn, E. R. (1994), *Imagery in Sports and Physical Performance*, Amityville, NY: Baywood Pub. Co.

4. Hunt, A. (2014), *Hopes for Great Happenings (Routledge Revivals)*, Routledge

10: Your Enjoyment

1. Deepak Chopra (2009), *The Ultimate Happiness Prescription: 7 Keys to Joy and Enlightenment*, New York, NY: Harmony Books

Resources

Whilst this book is about longer-term strategies for developing your emotional health, there may be times when you need immediate support in a crisis.

The following helplines and organisations are available within the UK at time of publication. You can find a directory of more specialist helplines at www.helplines. org/helplines

A further list of resources – including international helplines – can be downloaded at www.nickhernbooks. co.uk/emotional-health-resources

CALM (Campaign Against Living Miserably)
www.thecalmzone.net
0800 585858 + livechat

MIND
www.mind.org.uk
Support line 0300 102 1234
Info line 0300 123 3393

Papyrus Prevention of Young Suicide
www.papyrus-uk.org
Hopeline 0800 068 4141

Samaritans
www.samaritans.org
116 123

SHOUT
www.giveusashout.org
Text 'SHOUT' to 85258

Centre for Mental Health
www.centreformentalhealth.org.uk

Mental Health Foundation
www.mentalhealth.org.uk

Rethink Mental Illness
www.rethink.org

Together
www.together-uk.org

NHS Talking Therapies
www.nhs.uk/service-search/mental-health/find-an-NHS-talking-therapies-service

About the Authors

Andy Barker

Andy has experience in the music industry, the film industry, the world of theatre, videogames, and learning and development. Highlights include working with Jim Henson's Muppets and with Andrew Lloyd Webber's numerous West End productions. Amongst a wide range of backstage credits, he was part of the original London productions of *Evita*, *Starlight Express* and *Chess*, transferred *Single Spies* from the National Theatre to the West End, enjoyed a run on *Me and My Girl* in London, and was Company Manager of the D'Oyly Carte Opera at the Savoy Theatre. He then moved into computer games and was part of the original team that took a videogames start-up through to becoming the European PlayStation division of Sony. Andy is a certified performance coach, trainer and author with a broad experience of corporate senior management. His other book, *Unlock You*, co-written with Beth Wood, was published by Pearson and shortlisted for Business Book of the Year in 2020.

> 'Part of my love of being a performance coach is the fulfilment I get from guiding individuals to discover solutions for the challenges they face. I have always sought out pioneering work environments where relationships are prioritised alongside goals. I have been fortunate to be "in the room when it happened" on key moments of genuine creative alchemy – I am so grateful for my diverse career and feel a sense of duty to pay back key insights. Mind Fitness is a company I am immensely proud of and together with Beth Wood and Brian Cooley, my two co-authors, we have built something unique in the learning and development space.'

Brian Cooley

Brian has always advocated for untold stories to be heard. He cites a key influence as training with Augusto Boal, the Brazilian creator of the Theatre of the Oppressed, at Goldsmiths University in 1987. As a performer, director and writer, highlights include work with Red Ladder, Sheffield Crucible, Theatr Clwyd, The Moving Picture Mime Show and Doctor Foster's Travelling Theatre. He is a qualified facilitator, performance coach, entrepreneur and co-author of several plays, training programmes and books (including this one!). His business experience as a C-Suite leader in the UK and USA, in both the private and public sectors, has given him a wealth of practical experience and insights to draw upon when working with organisations or individuals to help unlock potential.

> 'My meaning and purpose have always been deeply connected with helping to empower others – I have found satisfaction in advocating and being an ally for disenfranchised groups. Systemic discrimination will continue until we reach the understanding that we are all diminished by inequality. It's up to us as individuals to act to right the wrongs that blight the lives of so many. This begins with us – the first person we lead is ourselves. Mind Fitness is on a mission to help engineer high functioning teams that can embrace diversity and engage in healthy conflict.'

Beth Wood

After training at Guildford School of Acting, Beth began in 'mainstream' theatre, directing in the West End, at regional theatres, and for numerous tours. From the outset she sat on committees, boards and leaders' panels advocating for equality, long-term health and creative diversity, working with arts organisations, councils and funding bodies. She was also a drama consultant for Surrey for eight years, designing and delivering work for young people with additional needs and specialist INSET sessions for teachers. Beth moved predominantly into inclusive theatre mid-career and was Artistic Director of Theatre

Exchange, Harlequin Outreach and the Arc, before founding Prospero Theatre in 2015. Beth is still Artistic Director of Prospero which is an inclusive company working with adults and young people with disabilities and mental health challenges. As a writer Beth has written more than sixty plays which have been performed by sixteen companies in five countries, the drama and editorial section for the Longmans Shakespeare Series, one novel (*Madelaine and the Forest*), and in 2019 co-wrote *Unlock You* with Andy Barker (shortlisted for Business Book of the Year 2020).

Beth is co-founder of Mind Fitness and now heads up its sister company, Mind Fitness for Performers. She works with drama schools, theatre companies and creative organisations to design and deliver training in mental and emotional health.

'I believe passionately in the creative potential of each and every person, and early on discovered the incredible power of mindfulness to take people to a place where the self-sabotage that is so common in our culture stops, and this potential can be tapped. Mindfulness is fused through all the creative work of Prospero and the training work I do with individuals, groups and online. I have worked through my life to create safe and nurturing environments where people can be their whole selves, continue to learn and develop, and discover the joy that comes from collective endeavour. I use the enormous power of the arts to campaign for a world in which every voice is valued.'

Index of Exercises

Exercises in **bold** are accompanied by worksheets in the workbook.

Exercises in *italics* are available as audio recordings.

www.nickhernbooks.co.uk/emotional-health-resources